Citizenship for the Future

A Practical Classroom Guide

David Hicks

To all those working for more just and sustainable futures

© **WWF-UK, 2001**

All rights reserved. The material in this book may be photocopied for non-commercial use within the purchasing education institution only. No reproduction, copy or transmission of this publication may otherwise be made, in whole or in part, without the prior written permission of the publishers.

Published by WWF-UK, Panda House, Weyside Park, Godalming, Surrey GU7 1XR.
WWF-UK registered charity number 1081247
A company limited by guarantee number 4016725
Panda device © 1986 WWF ® WWF registered trademark owner

A catalogue record for this book is available from The British Library

ISBN 1 85850 174 1

Designed by Gecko Limited

Printed by Lamport Gilbert Ltd., Reading

WWF-UK gratefully acknowledges the kind co-operation of the many individuals, organisations and companies who have allowed us to reprint material in this publication. We apologise to those who, despite our best efforts, we have been unable to contact, and welcome any advice or information that would assist us in ensuring that appropriate credits can be added to future editions.

Also by David Hicks

Minorities: A Teacher's Resource Book for the Multi-ethnic Curriculum

Teaching World Studies: An Introduction to Global Perspectives in the Curriculum (with Charles Townley)

World Studies 8–13: A Teacher's Handbook (with Simon Fisher)

Education for Peace: Issues, Principles and Practice in the Classroom

Making Global Connections: A World Studies Workbook (with Miriam Steiner)

Preparing for the Future: Notes and Queries for Concerned Educators

Visions of the Future: Why we Need to Teach for Tomorrow (with Cathie Holden)

Futures Education: The World Yearbook of Education 1998 (with Richard Slaughter)

Contents

PART THREE • Teacher Support

8 Taking Things Further

Preface

If all education is for the future, then the future needs to be a more explicit concern in education. In the first decade of the 21st century, the current state of the planet guarantees a future very different from today. What are the implications of this for citizenship education – now a central concern in schooling? To study only the problems of society can be an alienating experience for pupils: they also need opportunities to explore what sort of future they want for themselves and society, and the action needed to help bring that future about.

For children in school now, adult life will stretch well into the latter part of the century. How the school curriculum can contribute to more futures-orientated thinking, in both the local and global community, is thus the focus of this book. Much of the innovative work in global education over the last quarter century focused on the need to teach about issues of global interdependence. Such interdependence also exists across time, however, and it is this temporal dimension that now requires equal attention. Much of the expertise on this is found in the field of futures education.

I would like to thank all those friends and colleagues who have supported my work in these and other fields over the last 20 years. My gratitude to the particular people who helped make this book possible can be found in the Acknowledgements.

David Hicks

THE PURPOSE AND STRUCTURE OF THIS BOOK

A new century and a new millennium represent a good time to be thinking about the future. The children we teach in school now will become the parents, voters, workers, business people and visionaries of tomorrow. From this generation will come the leaders of the early and mid 21st century. When and where in the education of young people do we help them look at the kind of future they want for themselves, for society and the planet?

What Alvin Toffler said about education still holds true today:

"All education springs from images of the future and all education creates images of the future. Thus all education, whether so intended or not, is a preparation for the future. Unless we understand the future for which we are preparing we may do tragic damage to those we teach." [1]

Forward-looking thinking

This book is intended for all those – teachers, parents, governors/school board members, inspectors and others – who believe that young people should be encouraged to explore their hopes and fears for the future of society and the planet. Based on the notion that developing skills of forward-looking thinking is vital in times of rapid national and global change, it provides an innovative and practical starting point for schools wishing to promote the notion of responsible global citizenship.

In particular the activities in this book are designed to help pupils:

- develop a more futures-orientated perspective on their own lives and events in the wider world
- identify and envision scenarios for the future which are more just and sustainable
- exercise their critical thinking skills and creative imagination more effectively
- participate in more thoughtful and informed decision making in the present
- engage in active and responsible citizenship in the local and global community on behalf of present and future generations.

This book is issue-based and intended to contribute to on-going work in personal and social education and citizenship as well as in other curriculum subjects. It is primarily intended for use with pupils in the 9-14 age range, although the ideas can, of course, be adapted for use with both younger and older age groups.

© Mark Edwards for WWF-UK

Part One provides the background and theoretical context for the practical activities, and sets out clearly their educational rationale and how they relate to curriculum subjects. Part Two, the bulk of the book, contains a range of detailed classroom activities, all of which help children to explore issues of citizenship in the 21st century. Some readers may wish to move straight to this section and come back to the opening chapters at their leisure. Part Three provides further information about useful resources and support for teachers.

Children's concerns

"My hopes for the future are to have a happy life and to live for a long time and have a nice family. And that my cat and goldfish will live for a long time..."

"I hope that in the future there will be no more war and hunger and the world will become green and everybody will care to make it better and the world will unite again."

"Another world fear is that the atmosphere will get too polluted so that we cannot live any longer."

These are the concerns of some 10-year olds from a Berkshire school. They range from the personal to the global; from their families and pets to the welfare of other people and the planet itself. Should we educate young people to unthinkingly accept the status quo or should we encourage them to reflect critically on the world in order to improve it? What does effective preparation for life in the 21st century look like in a multicultural society and an interdependent world?

Research from many countries shows that young people are keenly interested in the sort of future they are likely to inherit. [2] They are concerned about a wide range of issues – from the personal to the global, and whilst they often fear that the future may be worse than today, they hope that they can contribute in some way to creating a *better* future. Research in the UK with a sample of pupils from both primary and secondary schools reveals an interesting picture of their concerns for the future. [3] These are summarised below.

Children's concerns for the future

Personal

- Getting a good job
- Health problems
- Doing well at school
- Money problems
- Good relationships
- Family problems

Local

- Crime and violence
- Jobs and employment
- Range of amenities
- Environmental threats

Global

- War and peace
- Environmental damage
- Poverty and hunger
- Relationships between countries
- Natural and human disasters

Whilst the importance of these issues varies somewhat with age and gender, all of these concerns are cited by pupils in the middle years of schooling. It is natural that children should be concerned both about the current state of the planet and also about the future. They are aware that there are many global issues which affect their lives now, and that the future holds both promise and threat. For young people, the future is everything since most of their lives still lie before them.

As children well know, their future adult life will be greatly affected by what is happening in the world today. It is important, therefore, for teachers and pupils to develop some critical sense of the current state of the world (where we are now) and also of future possibilities (where we want to get to).

A CHOICE OF FUTURES

The beginning of a new century often feels like the crossing of a threshold – but to what? What do we want to leave behind in the old century and what to take forward? Where are we going and does this bear any relationship to where we'd like to go? What does a better world look like? And for whom would it be better? If we are to avoid curricula that are merely nationalistic, such questions must begin with the current state of the planet – in our own communities and globally.

State of the world

At the start of the 21st century the global scene continues to shift and change, with new and violent ethnic conflicts; debates about the ethics of biotechnology; the continuing economic gap between global North and South; further damage to the environment; continuing sexual inequality and racial injustice. Local and global issues mirror each other and are inextricably interconnected.

The 1999-2000 edition of *Vital Signs: The Environmental Trends that are Shaping our Future* [4] reports that:

- there has been a further increase in the Earth's average temperature which has contributed to record weather-related damage from storms and floods
- the growth of wind and solar energy sources now greatly exceeds that of fossil fuels
- future world food supplies may currently be less secure than at any time in recent history
- the share of national populations linked to the Internet ranges from 1 in 4 in the USA, 1 in 800 in China, to 1 in 2,100 in India and 1 in 4,000 in Africa

- world population is now 6 billion and the projected UN figure for 2050 is 9 billion
- many insects/diseases are developing a resistance to once effective pesticides, and public resistance to genetically modified crops is increasing in both richer and poorer countries.

The Western economic model

"The Western economic model – the fossil-fuel based, automobile centred, throwaway economy – that so dramatically raised living standards for part of humanity during this century is in trouble... The shift to an environmentally sustainable economy may be as profound a transition as the Industrial Revolution that led to the current dilemma was."

Source: Brown, L et al (1999) State of the World 1999, Earthscan

Problems of inequality, injustice, environmental damage and violence are all present in our own communities as well as on a global scale. Increasingly it is recognised that they cannot be seen as separate problems: they are, rather, part of an overall global crisis involving our notions of economy, technology, welfare, environment and ways of relating to each other. It is this crisis, and our attempts to resolve it, which will drastically affect the lives of present and future generations.

In part this relates to the process of globalisation which is changing the world before our very eyes. Put simply, globalisation is about the growing number of linkages in our lives that bind local and global communities more closely together: it is about the multiplicity of interconnections which increasingly link all parts of the world, for example trade, finance, knowledge, communications, culture, crime, drugs, fashion, beliefs. This web of connections results in local-global interdependence [5] as events and decisions in one part of the world impact on distant places in ways that would once have been inconceivable. As a result of these deep-seated changes, the current world order is in a process of transformation so extensive that it even challenges the primacy of the nation state.

The consequences of globalisation are contradictory. On the one hand these forces lead to greater *integration*, for example the European Union, transnational corporations, international airports, pop music, consumerism, fashion. At the same time globalisation is helping create an opposing tendency, that of *fragmentation*, for example the resurgence of nationalism; breakaway states and regions; issues of ethnic and religious identity; new social movements that challenge the old order over issues such as the environment, human rights, gender equality and third world debt. It is no wonder that these mutually opposing tendencies cause extreme turbulence in our daily lives and the global system. The times that we live in are by definition contradictory, complex and uneven.

The origins of this turmoil lie in the assumptions we hold and the structures we have created in the Western world for managing economics, society and the environment. [6] One way of challenging these assumptions and structures is by asking questions about what sort of future we want for ourselves and for others.

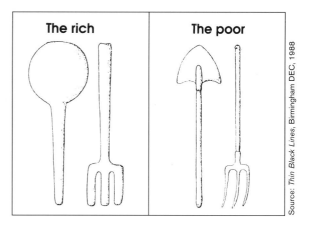

| The rich | The poor |

Source: *Thin Black Lines*, Birmingham DEC, 1988

Alternative futures

A new century and a new millennium present us with an opportunity to re-examine ourselves, our values and institutions, how we feel about the world we have inherited, and what sort of world we wish to help create. Educators have a crucial role to play in asking such critical questions about the future. [7]

The images that we have of the future matter because they help determine our priorities in the present. Such images play a critical role in the creation of change. They exert a powerful influence over what people think is, or is not, worth doing in the present. It is important to recall here that there is no such thing as the future (singular), for at any given moment in time any number of futures (plural) could possibly come about. The term 'alternative futures' is thus used in this book as a shorthand reminder of this.

It is important at this point to recall that different people may have quite different views of the future. Consider the different perspectives that a child in London, a single parent in Wales, a worker in Dresden or a mother in Brazil might have. Clearly some groups have much more power in society than others to define and create the future, generally those who are rich in the global system or who wield power through, say, transnational corporations, international banking, governments, advertising, the media. In one sense such powerful groups also 'colonise' the future, particularly big business with its constant creation of new 'needs' to ensure that their goods will sell tomorrow.

Every culture has its dream, whether religious or secular, of a past or future better world. In Western thought this aspiration has become known as utopia. Utopias are blueprints for a better future society and utopians may present their ideas as fiction, where the ideal society is set in some other time or place, or as an actual programme for political and social change.

Clearly utopias reflect the age in which they were conceived, but they always have a double-edged message: a critique of what is wrong with present society and a vision of what a better society would look like. Literary utopias range from Plato's *Republic* and Thomas Moore's *Utopia* to William Morris's famous *News from Nowhere* and Marge Piercy's *Woman on the Edge of Time*. Many groups have also planned and set up their own utopian communities with varying degrees of success: Gerrard Winstanley and the Diggers in the 17th century; religious groups such as the Shakers in the 18th century; and working communities such as Robert Owen's at New Lanark in the 19th century.

> *"Progress is the realisation of Utopias."*
>
> Source: Oscar Wilde

In his study of the famous writer, designer and political activist William Morris, Stephen Coleman writes:

"The utopian imagination, at its most radical, invades the prevailing concept of reality, undermines certainties about what humans must always be like, and casts doubt on the inevitabilities of the relations of everyday life." [8]

This long-standing and vital tradition can continue to inspire critical action for change and nourish our creative imaginations today. It gives food for thought when exploring issues to do with self, society and responsible citizenship.

A SUSTAINABLE SOCIETY

Key features

The most essential element in any notion of a preferable future has to be that of sustainable development – the major focus of concern at the Earth Summit in 1992. Here, actions needed to preserve the world's environment, reduce inequalities and achieve sustainable development were discussed and agreed, and set out in Agenda 21 – a plan for the 21st century. When the British government signed Agenda 21, it committed itself to sustainable development and recognised the importance of education to the process. Indeed education for sustainable development (ESD) is now an integral part of the National Curriculum for England. [9]

Traditional ideas of progress and development narrowly focus on economic growth (GNP as a measure of consumption) with its intrinsic discounting of other 'costs'. There are three major disadvantages to this 'normal' system of accounting: i) some people benefit at the expense of others; ii) people benefit at the expense of the environment; and iii) people today benefit at the expense of future generations. On this basis such models of progress and development are clearly *unsustainable*.

In contrast *sustainable* development prioritises equally the welfare of both people and planet. It emphasises: i) increased levels of social and economic well-being, particularly for the least advantaged in society; ii) increased emphasis on the protection of the biosphere on which all life ultimately depends; and iii) that future generations should inherit at least as much wealth, natural and person-made, as we ourselves inherited.

Working towards a more sustainable society requires production planned to meet human needs together with a more just distribution of resources. It means reducing the harmful effects of industry and technology; challenging company policies which are dangerous to people and the environment; stopping old programmes which are inappropriate and damaging; reducing over-consumption and waste; restraining population growth; distinguishing clearly between wants and needs; and organising locally, nationally and globally for appropriate change.

There are many signs of such changes occurring: international agreements over global warming; politicians turning various shades of green; local national and international groups campaigning on poverty, peace, human rights and the environment; individuals looking more carefully at what they buy and consume; schools increasingly promoting active citizenship in the local community. [10]

Changing worldviews

Over the last 20 years many writers and commentators have argued that we are witnessing a major shift of worldview in economically developed countries. The worldview that has dominated Western society for several centuries is that of the Enlightenment and the Scientific and Industrial Revolutions. This view includes:

"... belief in the scientific method as the only approach to knowledge; the view of the universe as a mechanical system composed of elementary material building blocks; the view of life in society as a competitive struggle for existence; and the belief in unlimited material progress to be achieved through economic and technological growth." [11]

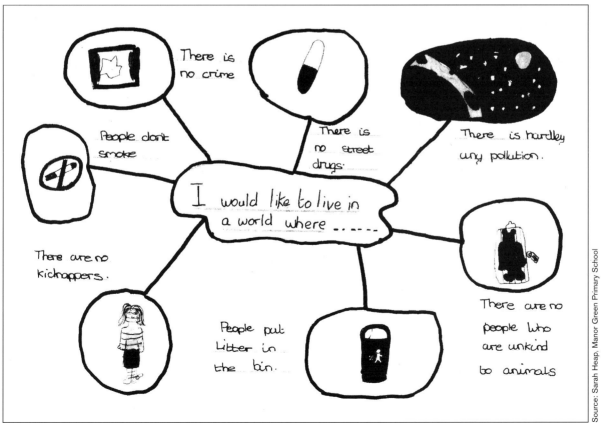

Source: Sarah Heap. Manor Green Primary School

We are now seeing an alternative 'story' or explanation emerging; a new belief paradigm with a quite different focus and emphasis. It explains 'reality' in a very different way, stressing a more holistic and less fragmented view of the universe. Such a change in emphasis is now apparent in many fields, ranging from the 'new' physics, ecology and healthcare, to philosophy, economics and biology.

Some of the main differences in emphasis are shown below, based on ideas developed in Milbrath's *Envisioning a Sustainable Society* and Inglehart's World Values surveys. [12] We live in a time of uncertainty and turbulence as these worldviews compete for our allegiance. The dominant mechanistic worldview of the last 300 years – with its emphasis on 'progress' at all costs – has brought innumerable benefits to a few but its basic assumptions have lead to the crisis of unsustainability. The emerging holistic worldview, with its emphasis on the welfare of people and planet, focuses on the revisioning of society that is needed to work towards a more sustainable future. We have a duty to help young people understand both these world views and their consequences for the future.

Changing worldviews

Dominant worldview	Emerging worldview
1 *Lower valuing of nature*	*Higher valuing of nature*
– human domination of nature to produce more goods – economic growth more important than environmental protection	– holistic relationship between humans and nature – environmental protection more important than economic growth
2 *Narrower compassion*	*Wider compassion*
– exploitation of other people and species – concern for this generation only	– concern for all people and species – concern also for future generations
3 *Risk always acceptable*	*Risk minimised by foresight*
– advances in science/technology always beneficial – emphasis on high technology	– greater social/political regulation to protect from high risk – emphasis on appropriate technology
4 *No limits to growth*	*Clear limits to growth*
– no real resource shortages – continued over-consumption	– many resources are finite – reduce, reuse and conserve
5 *Present society works well*	*Society needs transforming*
– competitive and hierarchical – complex and fast lifestyles	– co-operation and participation – simpler, more reflective lifestyles
6 *Old politics*	*New politics*
– often opposes pressure groups – traditional left-right spectrum	– pressure groups act as vital antennae for society – a more participatory democracy

At the heart of citizenship education lies the welfare of the individual, others, society and the environment and correspondingly the responsibilities that each requires of the other. To understand that there is not one single future but various possible futures highlights the need to make choices between alternatives. The current state of global society requires that exploration of just and sustainable futures becomes a major priority at all levels of education. Future generations would surely ask no less of us than this. Current support for global citizenship now provides the opportunity.

Source: Nigel Paige

2 | Citizenship Education

EXPLORING SELF AND SOCIETY

One of the central aims of education has to be with exploring the nature of our common humanity. What does it mean to be fully human? What rights and responsibilities follow from this? How do we as teachers stay open to both the joy and pain that lie at the heart of the human condition? And how do we help pupils better understand both self and society? These are some of the fundamental questions that each new generation needs to explore.

In England, current guidance states that:

"The school curriculum should contribute to the development of pupils' sense of identity through knowledge and understanding of the spiritual, moral, social and cultural heritages of Britain's diverse society and of the local, national... and global dimensions of their lives... the curriculum should [also] enable pupils to think creatively and critically, to solve problems and to make a difference for the better. It should give them the opportunity to become creative, innovative, enterprising and capable of leadership to equip them for their future lives as workers and citizens." [1]

Similarly, in Scotland, the 5–14 National Guidelines observe that:

"Schools, parents and society care that young people succeed in terms of attaining the knowledge, skills and, in time, qualifications required for a personally rewarding life, productive employment and active citizenship. Equally, they care that young people develop into healthy, fair-minded, considerate and responsible human beings. The school experience should play a major role in this development." [2]

This book is specifically designed to support such broad curriculum aims and does so in three interrelated ways. Firstly, it focuses on the strengthened status of citizenship within schooling. Secondly, it highlights the need for this to involve a clear futures perspective. Thirdly, it draws attention to the urgent need for education for sustainable development.

"Every second we live is a new and unique moment of the universe, a moment that was never before and never will be again. And what do we teach our children in school? We teach them that 2 and 2 make 4, and that Paris is the capital of France. We should say to each of them, 'Do you know what you are? You are a marvel. You are unique. In the millions of years that have passed, there has never been another child like you.'"

Source: Pablo Casals

Citizenship

Citizenship education should be seen as of crucial importance throughout the entire years of schooling. This in increasingly recognised in the different curricula of the UK:

"Citizenship gives pupils the knowledge, skills and understanding to play an effective role in society at local, national and international levels. It helps them to become informed, thoughtful and responsible citizens who are aware of their duties and rights. It promotes their spiritual, moral, social and cultural development, making them more self-confident and responsible both in and beyond the classroom. It encourages pupils to play a helpful part in the life of their schools, neighbourhoods, communities and the wider world." [3]

"Education for citizenship is important because every society needs people who can contribute effectively, in a variety of ways, to the future health and wellbeing of communities and the environment, locally, nationally and globally. Fostering active and responsible citizens contributes to the process of developing a healthy and vibrant culture of democratic participation." [4]

Whilst clearly there are differences of emphasis for each age group, it is possible to identify a core set of *ideas* which are as follows:

- the nature of human rights and responsibilities
- diversity of national, religious and ethnic identities

- the workings of parliament, central and local government
- the role of voluntary, community and pressure groups
- the role and significance of the media in society
- the interdependence of the local-global community.

Similarly it is possible to identify a core set of *skills* to be developed over the years of schooling:

- justifying a personal opinion about issues
- contributing to discussion and debate
- analysing information and its sources
- empathising with other people's experiences
- resolving differences by exploring alternatives
- participating responsibly in school/the local community.

Source: Nigel Paige

Citizenship education draws on two long-standing educational traditions. The first is the humanistic learner-centred tradition that focuses on the development and fulfilment of each individual. The second is concerned with building greater equality in society by highlighting and challenging existing inequalities, for example in relation to race, class, gender, age and disability. In his book *Daring to be a Teacher*, Robin Richardson writes:

> *"Both traditions are concerned with wholeness and holistic thinking, but neither, arguably, is complete without the other. There cannot be wholeness in individuals independently of strenuous attempts to heal rifts and contradictions in wider society and in the education system. Conversely, political struggle to create wholeness in society – that is, equality and justice in dealings and relationships between social classes, between countries, between ethnic groups, between women*

> *and men – is doomed to no more than partial success and hollow victories, at best, if it is not accompanied by, and if it does not in its turn strengthen and sustain, the search for wholeness and integration in individuals."* [5]

Education for sustainable development

To the above can now be added a third tradition which has its roots in environmental education and development education. As the first chapter highlighted, there is now an urgent need to work towards a more sustainable future in relation to the welfare of both people and planet.

Environmental education has a 30 year international history and has traditionally focused on issues relating to care of the biosphere at both local and global scales. Development education (and also world studies or global education) has a similarly long history and draws attention in particular to issues of human welfare. As mentioned in the first chapter, the Earth Summit in 1992 highlighted the interrelationship between environmental welfare and human welfare (people and planet). The term education for sustainable development is used to embrace both these concerns, bringing together social, environmental and economic considerations.

In Chapter 36 of Agenda 21, education is described as being critical for:

> *"promoting sustainable development and improving the capacity of the people to address environment and development issues. It is critical for achieving environmental and ethical awareness, values, attitudes, skills and behaviour consistent with sustainable development and for effective public participation and decision-making."*

In the UK, the various curriculum review processes include an exploration of how education for sustainable development might be implemented at all levels of education. In Scotland, such concerns have long been evident in the curriculum, for example through Environmental Studies 5-14, which attempts not only to develop pupils' knowledge, skills and understanding, but also to develop informed attitudes so that:

"Pupils gain wider knowledge, experience and understanding of the world in which they live ... [They will also] begin to appreciate differences in ways of thinking, working and viewing the world. They will gradually develop attitudes informed by understanding of social and environmental issues." [6]

The ideas indentified as being central to developing informed attitudes include:

- responsible citizenship
- sustainable development and interdependence
- social equity and diversity
- conflicts of interest in the social, physical and natural environment
- Moral and ethical considerations arising from scientific, social and technological change.

The revised National Curriculum for England also now draws attention to the importance of this aspect of the wider curriculum. In a new section covering the values, purposes and aims of education, it recognises that:

"Education is a route to equality of opportunity for all, a healthy and just democracy, a productive economy and sustainable development."

As part of preparing pupils for the opportunities, responsibilities and experiences of life, it states that the curriculum should:

"develop [pupils'] awareness and understanding of, and respect for, the environments in which they live, and secure their commitment to sustainable development at a personal, local, national and global level. It should equip [pupils] to make informed choices at school and throughout their lives."

Additionally, the section 'Promoting other aspects of the school curriculum' includes education for sustainable development which, it says:

"enables pupils to develop the knowledge, skills, understanding and values to participate in decisions about the way we do things individually and collectively, both locally and globally, that will improve the quality of life now without damaging the planet for the future." [7]

AN INTERNATIONAL CONCERN

It would be wrong to think that an interest in citizenship education is solely a UK concern. The turbulence in the world community, referred to in Chapter 1, has thrown up a variety of questions about identity, rights, nationality and responsibilities at local and national levels. Many initiatives in citizenship education are thus underway. For example, the National Foundation for Educational Research (NFER) has been involved since 1994 in a study approved by the International Association for the Evaluation of Educational Achievement (IEA), which means that developments in citizenship in the UK can be judged within an international frame of reference. [8]

One of the most valuable NGO (non-governmental organisation) initiatives has come from the education team at Oxfam which consulted widely with experts in the field to produce a curriculum framework for global citizenship. [9] Extracts from this can be found in the Appendix, but the key elements are set out below:

Key elements of global citizenship

Knowledge and understanding
- social justice and equity
- peace and conflict
- globalisation and interdependence
- cultural diversity
- sustainable development

Skills
- co-operation and conflict resolution
- critical thinking

- ability to argue effectively
- ability to challenge injustice and inequality

Values and attitudes
- sense of identity and self-esteem
- empathy
- value and respect for diversity
- commitment to social justice and equity
- concern for environment and sustainable development
- belief that people can make a difference

This checklist succinctly highlights the key elements required in any global approach to citizenship. Interestingly, these 'elements' are also identified as key to education for sustainable development.

A further example of wider initiatives comes from the Citizenship Education Policy Study (CEPS) project, an international research network set up to examine the changing character of citizenship over the next 25 years and the implications of such changes for educational policy. [10] The countries involved are England, USA, Germany, Greece, Hungary, Netherlands, Canada, Japan and Thailand. In describing the findings of this research project, John Cogan and Ray Derricott talk about the need for 'multidimensional citizenship'. The team of international experts that they consulted reached consensus on eight competencies or characteristics which citizens of the 21st century will need to possess:

Key citizen characteristics

- looking at problems in a global context
- working co-operatively and responsibly
- accepting cultural differences
- thinking in a critical and systemic way
- solving conflicts non-violently
- changing lifestyles to protect the environment
- defending human rights
- participating in politics

The framework proposed by Cogan and Derricott for developing and promoting these citizen characteristics is outlined in the following section.

FOUR DIMENSIONS OF CITIZENSHIP

Given the complexities of life in the early 21st century, it is essential that any notion of citizenship and citizenship education be as holistic as possible, thus the research team's focus on 'multidimensional' citizenship. They write:

"This term is intended to describe the complex, multifaceted conceptualisation of citizenship and citizenship education that will be needed if citizens are to cope with the challenges... we will face in the early decades of the 21st century". [11]

Four dimensions are identified each of which provide useful categories for policy analysis and recommendation.

The personal dimension

Citizenship must always begin, as Robin Richardson argues above, with the individual's search for integration and wholeness. Thus building self-esteem, learning to work co-operatively, identifying one's personal stance on an issue and developing interpersonal skills are all essential prerequisites for developing a sense of oneself within society. It is during this on-going quest for positive self-identity that particular attitudes and values will be internalised about oneself and others. The personal dimension of citizenship must thus explicitly address issues of ethics and values whilst recognising that these may sometimes be culturally variable. At a personal level, therefore, there needs to be developed a predisposition to act in accordance with the 'Key citizen characteristics' shown above. The skills and values needed in order to do this are those listed under the 'Key elements of global citizenship'. It is clear from this of course that these principles of citizenship education need to infuse the whole ethos of a school.

requires mutual respect for ethnic, religious and national diversity. Participation in society thus has a much wider connotation than just the right to vote. The betterment of society requires that each generation reviews both the assets it has inherited from the past, both natural and human-made, and what action needs to be taken to safeguard the rights of future generations. Thus citizen involvement in new social movements focusing on issues such as gender, the environment, disability, poverty and war, is often at the leading edge of social change. Clear visions of a preferred future (see Chapter 5) can help guide such action for change.

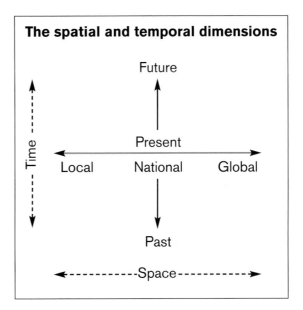

The spatial and temporal dimensions

The spatial dimension

Given the multiple communities to which we now all belong – local, regional, national and global – it is clear that citizenship education has a strong spatial component. Whereas once the curricula of the UK focused on Britain, western Europe and the Commonwealth, this no longer reflects the reality of world politics. Not only do the local, national and international demand equal attention but, more importantly, they are also inextricably related, making global interdependence one of the key features of the new century. Many of today's problems transcend national boundaries and require international co-operation for their resolution. But at the same time as we become more

---

Questions to ask about an issue

i) *What is the issue?*

What do we think, feel, hope and fear, in relation to this particular issue? What do others who are involved think, feel and say?

ii) *How has it come about?*

Why do we and others think, feel and act the way we do? What and who have influenced us and others involved? What is the history of this situation?

iii) *Who gains, who loses?*

Who has the power in this situation and how do they use it? Is it used to the advantage of some and the disadvantage of others? If so, in what way?

iv) *What is our vision?*

What would things look like in a more just, peaceful and sustainable future, for ourselves and for others? What values will we use to guide our choices?

v) *What can be done?*

What are the possible courses of action open to us? What are others already doing? Which course of action is most likely to achieve our vision of a preferred future?

vi) *How will we do it?*

How shall we implement our plan of action in school, at home, or in the community? How shall we work together? Whose help might we need? How do we measure our success?

The social dimension

The social dimension of citizenship recognises that our identity and sense of self only comes about through interaction with others. Being able to work with others in the successful resolution of conflict and the identification and achievement of chosen goals is at the heart of good citizenship education. Indeed it is an essential survival skill in any community or society and further global in perspective we look more locally for our roots and our sense of identity. Global education is the term used internationally to highlight this need for a local-global perspective in the curriculum. [12] It has to be an essential element in any notion of citizenship education as the curriculum framework proposed by Oxfam also recognises (see Appendix).

The temporal dimension

The issues that we are faced with in the present cannot be fully understood or acted on responsibly unless set in the wider temporal context of past, present and future. All issues in the present, from the most personal to the global, have their origins firmly in time past. Exploring the question

---

The educational rationale for a futures dimension in the curriculum

1 Pupil motivation

Pupil expectation about the future can affect behaviour in the present, for example that something is, or is not, worth working for. Clear images of desired personal goals can help stimulate motivation and achievement.

2 Anticipating change

Anticipatory skills and flexibility of mind are important in times of rapid change. Such skills enable pupils to deal more effectively with uncertainty and to initiate, rather than merely respond to, change.

3 Critical thinking

In weighing up information, considering trends and imagining alternatives, pupils will need to exercise reflective and critical thinking. This is often triggered by realising the contradictions between how the world is now and how one would like it to be.

4 Clarifying values

All images of the future are underpinned by differing value assumptions about human nature and society. In a democratic society pupils need to begin to identify such value judgements before they can themselves make appropriate choices between alternatives.

5 Decision making

Becoming more aware of trends and events which are likely to influence one's future and investigating the possible consequences of one's actions on others in the future, leads to more thoughtful decision making in the present.

6 Creative imagination

One faculty that can contribute to, and which is particularly enhanced by, designing alternative futures is that of the creative imagination. Both this and critical thinking are needed to envision a range of preferable futures from the personal to the global.

7 A better world

It is important in a democratic society that young people develop their sense of vision, particularly in relation to more just and sustainable futures. Such forward-looking thinking is an essential ingredient in both the preserving and improving of society.

8 Responsible citizenship

Critical participation in democratic life leads to the development of political skills and thus more active and responsible citizenship. Future generations are then more likely to benefit, rather than lose, from decisions made today.

9 Stewardship

Understanding the short and long-term consequences of current local and global trends, as well as the action needed to change these, can lead to a sense of stewardship both for the planet now and for those yet to come.

'Where are we now?' requires that we also consider the related question 'Where have we come from?' These questions are as pertinent to issues of racial abuse and sexual harassment in the playground as they are to nuclear safety and global warming. They equally require a third question which is 'Where do we want to get to?', that is what would a satisfactory outcome look like for these and other issues. In relation to the temporal dimension it is an explicit futures perspective which is most often missing from the curriculum. Futures education is the term used internationally to highlight the need for more futures-orientated thinking in schools, not about the future of education *per se* but rather about the wider future of society. [13]

Telling lies to the young is wrong.

Proving to them that lies are true is wrong.

Telling them that god's in his heaven

and all's well with the world is wrong.

The young know what we mean.

The young are people.

Tell them the difficulties can't be counted,

and let them see not only what will be

but see with clarity these present times.

Say obstacles exist they must encounter,

sorrow happens, hardship happens.

The hell with it. Who never knew

the price of happiness will not be happy.

Forgive no error you recognise,

it will repeat itself, increase

and afterwards our pupils

will not forgive us what we forgave.

Yevgeny Yevtushenko

Source: 'Lies' from *Selected Poems Yevtushenko*, translated by Robin Milner-Gulland and Peter Levi, Penguin, 1962. © Robin Milner-Gulland and Peter Levi, 1962. Reproduced by permission of Penguin Books Ltd.

The various classroom activities set out in Part Two of this book, together with the introductions to each of the chapters, give a good sense of the 'what' and 'how' in particular of the futures dimension in citizenship. The activity chapters follow a logical sequence, although it is not expected that they will all be worked through in detail, rather that activities will be selected to enhance on-going work in the curriculum.

'Thinking about the Future' (Chapter 4) sets the scene. It begins in the 'here and now' and invites pupils to begin contemplating the future. It provides an initial introduction to the notion of alternative futures and in particular probable futures. In 'Envisioning the Future' (Chapter 5), children identify their own preferable futures, for themselves and for society more widely. Then in 'Choosing the Future' (Chapter 6), different scenarios for the future are offered for exploration and discussion. The final activities in 'A Sustainable Future' (Chapter 7) explore the notion of sustainability through case studies on projects for change, energy, transport and global warming.

3 | A Futures Perspective

This chapter considers the main subjects within the school curriculum to show how each can contribute to more futures-orientated thinking within citizenship education. Taken together these elements provide the basis for an explicit futures perspective across the school curriculum. This in turn begins to correct the 'temporal imbalance' caused by the frequent neglect of futures issues. Without such a perspective, the curriculum is failing to give pupils their full entitlement to preparation for adult life.

FUTURES-ORIENTATED THINKING

What is meant then by the term 'futures-orientated thinking'? In essence it involves the development of five basic life skills which are central to citizenship education. These are described in sequence in 'Futures skills' below. The activities set out in Chapters 4 to 7 are all designed to help develop these skills.

On the one hand it could be argued that this list merely epitomises the importance of developing transferable skills, and this is certainly true. At the same time these skills, as set out here, highlight what is needed to make more futures-orientated thinking a reality in the curriculum.

More broadly it is also possible to identify a range of concerns which futures-orientated thinking will embrace. These are summarised in 'Elements of a futures perspective' (over). A futures perspective in the curriculum will thus be marked by i) exploration of these themes; ii) development of these skills; iii) through active and experiential learning. Without a clear futures perspective citizenship will fail in its task of preparing young people effectively for adult life.

Futures skills

1 Anticipating the future

Most people are aware of the value of hindsight, the ability to look back on a situation and to learn from experience. As important as learning from the past is the ability to anticipate the future. Living in a rapidly changing world requires the development of foresight, the ability to scan ahead in order to minimise possible hazards and dangers.

2 Accepting consequences

Everything that we choose to do, for example, what we buy and consume, has consequences for ourselves, for others and for the environment. Some consequences, for example of dropping litter in the playground, are immediately apparent, but the consequences of many life choices occur elsewhere in time and space so that we do not see the results of our actions.

3 Envisioning alternatives

When considering how any situation might develop in the future it is important to consider a variety of alternative scenarios, whether personal, local or global. This helps to make clearer the range of possible options one might be faced with. It can also help in distinguishing between probable and preferable futures, and in clarifying the nature of the latter.

4 Making wiser choices

The value of using future scenarios is that one is able to choose from a wider range of options than is often the case. For each scenario one needs to ask: What are the benefits and disbenefits? And for whom? Scenarios are specifically designed to enhance this process of weighing things up so that better and wiser choices can then be made in the present.

5 Taking responsible action

Truly responsible citizenship can only come about as a result of exercising the first four skills of foresight, accepting consequences, envisioning alternatives and making wise choices. This in turn leads to the ability to take responsible action, whether in one's personal life, in the local community or in the wider world.

Elements of a futures perspective

1 State of the world

At the beginning of the new century, the state of the world continues to give cause for concern. Issues to do with the environment, wealth and poverty, peace and conflict, and human rights all have a major impact both locally and globally. Pupils need to know about the causes of such problems, how they will affect their lives, and the action needed to help resolve them.

2 Managing change

In periods of rapid social and technological change the past cannot provide an accurate guide to the future. Anticipation and adaptability, foresight and flexibility, innovation and intuition, become increasingly essential tools for survival. Pupils need to develop such skills in order to become more adaptable and pro-active towards change.

3 Views of the future

People's views of the future may vary greatly depending, for example, on age, gender, class and culture, as well as their attitudes to change, the environment and technology. Pupils need to be aware of how views of the future thus differ and the ways in which this affects people's priorities in the present.

4 Alternative futures

At any point in time a range of different futures is possible. It is useful to distinguish between probable futures – those which seem likely to come about, and preferable futures – those we feel *should* come about. Pupils need to explore a range of probable and preferable futures, from the personal and local to the global.

5 Hopes and fears

Hopes and fears for the future often influence decision making in the present. Fears can lead to the avoidance of problems rather than their resolution. Clarifying hopes for the future often enhances motivation in the present and thus positive action for change. Pupils need to explore their own hopes and fears for the future and learn to work creatively with them.

6 Past/present/future

Interdependence exists across both space and time. Past, present and future are inextricably connected. We are directly linked back in time by the oldest members of the community and forward nearly a century by those born today. Pupils need to explore these links and to gain a sense of both continuity and change, as well as of responsibility for the future.

7 Visions for the future

The transition from one century to another, and particularly from one millennium to another, is often seen as a turning point for society. What needs to be left behind and what taken forward? Visions of a better future can help to motivate active and responsible citizenship in the present. Pupils therefore need to develop their skills of envisioning and use of the creative imagination.

8 Future generations

Economists, philosophers and international lawyers increasingly recognise the rights of future generations. It has been suggested that no generation should inherit less human and natural wealth than the one that preceded it. Pupils need to discuss the rights of future generations and what the responsibility to uphold them may involve.

9 Sustainable futures

Current consumerist lifestyles on this planet are increasingly seen as unsustainable, often causing more damage than benefit. A sustainable society would prioritise concern for the environment, the poorest members of the community and the needs of future generations. Pupils need to understand how this applies to their everyday lives and possible future employment.

10 Competing worldviews

Worldviews are the 'stories' societies create to explain how the world works. In the West there is a clash between the old scientific/mechanistic view of the world, and an emerging environmental/holistic paradigm, which stresses a holistic and ecological worldview. Pupils need the opportunity to explore such competing worldviews and their implications for the future.

The suggestions that follow in these pages highlight the contributions that most subjects can make to citizenship education and education for sustainable development. They can be applied to curriculum planning both in specific subject areas and within wider topic work, whether at primary or secondary level.

CURRICULUM LINKS

English/Language

Speaking and listening can involve speculation about possible alternative futures and also discussion about the future consequences of decisions or actions made in the present. This requires the development of reasoned arguments; the ability to express a viewpoint; consideration of alternatives; and evaluating appropriate action, both individually and in group discussion.

Sources of information about the future come in many forms, from newspapers and magazines to stories and reference books. Two major contributions to a futures perspective from reading are, first, the study of fiction which looks at possible future worlds and societies and, secondly, the reading that is needed to research information about different possible futures. Reference books on global issues abound and there is a growing emphasis in them on the need to think more carefully about the future. In particular such resources need to be read critically: what sort of future do they assume?

Future worlds

Having studied a popular children's story about life in a future world, pupils compare the social organisation portrayed then with today. Which do they prefer and why? What are the advantages and disadvantages of each? Working in small groups they then compare their responses and together prepare a short group report to present to the whole class.

In reporting about futures issues in citizenship a variety of opportunities arise for promoting writing. Examples would include extracts from future diaries; letters written to or from people of the future; reports and stories about different futures, and future newspaper headlines and articles.

In drama small group improvisation can be used to explore future situations and dilemmas or the future consequences of choices made in the present. Media education has a vital role to play in the deconstruction of images of the future. TV, radio, films, videos, photographs, advertisements, newspapers and magazines often promote consumerist high-tech images of the future which need constant critical attention.

Schools for the 21st century

"Students in the next century will need to know how to create a civilisation that runs on sunlight, conserves energy, preserves biodiversity, protects soils and forests, develops sustainable local economies and restores the damage inflicted on the Earth. In order to achieve such ecological education we need to transform our schools and universities."

Source: David Orr, 'Schools for the 21st century', *Resurgence*, No 160, September/October 1993

Mathematics

The choice of problems to investigate in maths and the data to be collected or analysed, can relate to local and global citizenship issues. Using and applying number and data handling are extremely relevant here. For example, data can be collected locally, or existing data used, to study population growth through statistics relating to births and deaths, environmental emissions from local factories or consumer habits in shops. More broadly, data can be collected and examined on acid rain or global warming, for example.

Traffic problems

Having carried out a local traffic survey and tabulated details of the volume, flow and nature of vehicles, pupils compare these with projected figures from the local planning office and consider the likely impact of such traffic flow increase on the community. Which forms of transport cause least environmental impact and how could they be promoted?

Much of the work done by government departments and by business and industry involves attempts to predict and gauge social and economic trends. The possible future of society, or of different aspects of society, is often mapped by the extrapolation of statistics, whether of wealth and poverty, unemployment, the growth of green consumerism or increased interest in renewable forms of energy. Interpreting such figures and attempting to predict from them is essential in creating scenarios of probable futures. Students also need to learn that statistics can be used to cover up the existence of inequality and injustice.

© Mark Edwards/Still Pictures

Science

Progress in science has lead to many benefits for society, but also many ethical dilemmas, whether in relation to animal experiments, pollution from cars or pesticides in the water supply. All have major implications for the future. Scientific enquiry requires that pupils develop the ability to ask questions, predict and hypothesise. These are essential skills for understanding the future consequences of their own, and others', actions. Far too often in the past the longer term social and environmental impacts of scientific and technological development have either been ignored or inappropriately minimised.

By studying life processes and living things, and looking at different materials and their properties, pupils gain knowledge which is vital for understanding the nature of the planet they live on. To value biodiversity and to protect and conserve it today is one of the greatest gifts we can give to future generations. When looking at physical processes, important questions can also be raised about the need for renewable energy sources and the importance of energy conservation.

Waste dump

Pupils put together a file of cuttings about a toxic or waste dump on the edge of town. They investigate the nature and sources of the different wastes and their likely impact over time on the local environment. What other alternatives are there to the present situation? They then draw up their own plan of action as a basis for lobbying local councillors.

Study of the impact of waste disposal over time on different environments can draw on local examples and more distant ones, such as the dumping of European toxic waste in third world countries. It can also lead to a consideration of why waste reduction is more important than recycling.

Design and technology

In design and technology subjects, the cycle of developing ideas, planning, making products and evaluating them, takes the pupil from the present to the future in a very concrete way. Developing, planning and communicating ideas immediately requires that students speculate about and investigate the need for something which, as yet, does not exist. Ideally this identification of needs should be related to issues of human welfare rather than those of a consumerist society.

Working with tools, equipment, materials and components to make quality products involves the creation of that which has previously only been imagined, an essential element in futures thinking. Deciding how well the item meets the needs of others and/or its social and economic implications – that is evaluating processes and products – completes the process and, in particular, requires consideration of unforeseen consequences of the design proposal.

Energy conservation

Pupils consider various initiatives aimed at reducing domestic energy consumption in the school and at home. They then research, plan and design some of the key features of an energy efficient house, including procedures for evaluating its overall effectiveness. How might such ideas be more widely promoted and what might be some of the wider and longer term consequences of such promotion?

Source: Hector Breeze

Guardian 25.9.86

Information and communication technology (ICT)

ICT can contribute to a futures perspective in two main ways. Firstly, it is an important source of information and support for the research that is required in any investigation relating to citizenship. Sources of data on local and national government, and on issues of human rights and sustainable development, for example, can be identified and organised to suit different purposes.

Secondly, ICT encourages pupils to use simulations and explore models in order to answer 'What if ...?' questions. Such questions are, of course, at the heart of futures-orientated thinking, both personal and social. They also lie at the heart of citizenship education, for example, what happens if this conflict cannot be resolved peacefully? What is likely to happen if this minority group continues to face overt discrimination? What are the different scenarios for insurance companies if global climate change continues?

Geography

Given the subject's concern with social, economic and environmental issues, it is excellently placed to consider many current trends and events that will have a major impact on the future. Thus using geographical enquiry pupils can explore the different views that people, including themselves, hold about topical geographical issues. They can also be encouraged to reflect on why places change – for example, through the closure of shops, the building of new houses or through conservation projects, and how they may change in the future – for example, through an increase in traffic or an influx of tourists. This is about exploring probable futures and, given the emphasis in geography on exploring attitudes and values, can be about preferable futures too.

Comparing levels of welfare in different parts of the world raises questions about how such inequalities may be changed in the future. A study of environmental change and sustainable development can help pupils to understand how people have the power to improve or damage the environment, and how decisions in the present affect the future quality of people's lives. It also invites involvement in projects working for sustainable change.

I'D LIKE TO GO TO THE EC COUNTRY WITH THE THICKEST OZONE LAYER

TRAVEL AGENT

GREECE   SPAIN

ITALY

Source: Hector Breeze

Development issues

Pupils discuss the nature of development and under-development based on case studies of different aid projects. Who gives aid to whom and for what reasons? Who benefits and who does not from such aid programmes? Pupils then evaluate these projects against a checklist they have drawn up which itemises the key features of sustainable development.

History

Many historical skills are precisely those needed for the examination of alternative futures. Thus developing a sense of time, being able to place events in chronological sequence, realising that actions and events have future consequences, and exploring continuity and change are all extremely relevant. Similarly historical interpretation helps pupils to realise that there can be various versions of historical events and that such interpretations can be used to serve social and political purposes. This applies as much to perceptions of the future as it does of the past, and can help ensure more critical and creative thinking about the future.

Changes

Pupils talk to grandparents or other older people in the community about the changes that they have seen in their lifetime. What has struck them most and what changes had the most impact on their lives? They also look at changes in the local community and record these on a timeline as part of a project on 'Reviewing the 20th century: a balance sheet'.

Art and design

The skills and insights developed through art and design are vital for thinking about alternative futures. The emphasis on stimulating pupils' imagination, creativity and inventiveness allows a wide range of ideas and feelings to be expressed. The development of imagination, intuition and visualisation, is also essential to forward-looking thinking. What roles might art, craft and design play in the creation of a better society?

Modern (foreign) languages

The learning of a modern language helps pupils think about the future in two main ways. First, there is the need for both oral and written work which clearly illustrate the use of future and conditional tenses. Pupils are likely to learn these most easily if they are talking about future events and issues, which are of direct interest to them. Oral work requires both responses, questions and statements to be made about future plans and future events. Second, the broader context of language acquisition is the child's own society, the relevant culture and country, and issues in the wider world. What does citizenship mean to members of other European countries and what do they learn in school about this?

Modern Studies

In Scotland, the 5–14 curriculum currently includes the following elements under the heading of 'People and Society': i) 'People and Needs in Society' which fosters understanding of individual and social needs, and the relationship to economic factors; ii) 'Rules, Rights and Responsibilities in Society' which considers individual and collective rights and responsibilities in a democratic society, and iii) 'Conflict and Decision Making in Society' which looks at conflict and decision making processes including the influence of the media.

Religious Education

Several common themes are present in RE syllabuses. These include the need for pupils to: i) develop an awareness of self and one's relationships with others; ii) explore the human experience and the meaning of life; iii) develop an awareness of the world around them; iv) explore the main rites of passage in life; v) explore ethical traditions which inspire human endeavour; and vi) explore various spiritual traditions. Festivals, ceremonies, myths, legends and rites of passage, all have a crucial part to play in explaining and celebrating our span of time on this planet. Developing a sense of awe and wonder at natural phenomenon can also help create a sense of stewardship for the planet and its peoples. What do different religious traditions say about the 'good society' and what visions do they have of a 'better world?'

Earth prayer

We join with the Earth and each other
To bring new life to the land
To restore the waters
To refresh the air

We join with the Earth and each other
To renew the forests
To care for the plants
To protect the creatures

We join with the Earth and each other
To celebrate the seas
To rejoice in the sunlight
To sing the song of the stars

We join with the Earth and each other
To recreate the human community
To promote justice and peace
To remember our children

We join with the Earth and each other
We join together as many and diverse
expressions of one loving mystery:
for the healing of the Earth
and the renewal of all life.

Source: Roberts, R and Amidon, E eds, *Earth Prayers*, Harper San Francisco, 1991

Citizenship for the future

Community

What sort of community would we ideally like to live in? What examples are there from the past of people trying to create their ideal community? What do we need to do in order to create a better community now and in the future?

A pluralist society

What hopes and fears for the future do different ethnic and cultural groups in Britain have? What does a future society based on racial justice and equality actually look like? What needs to be done to achieve it?

Being a citizen

What does global citizenship look like and how does it relate to the local community? What rights and responsibilities should we have in the future? What rights should future generations have?

The family

What might the family look like in the future? What are the advantages and disadvantages of different forms of relating? How should we prepare for our future roles as parents and partners?

Democracy in action

What would a participatory democracy look like, in school, in the community and nationally? How can we really experience this? How might democracy evolve in the future?

The citizen and the law

What new legislation might be needed in order to create a more just and sustainable future? What sort of work, and what sort of leisure activities, promote environmental concern?

Work, employment and leisure

What sort of work and leisure would we like in the future? What sort of work, and what sort of leisure activities promote environmental concern?

Public services

What existing services support our visions of a better community? What new services are needed to help bring our preferable futures about? How might they be provided?

4 Thinking about the Future

INTRODUCTION

Most of the activities suggested in this book are based on active learning in small groups. This requires, and will help pupils develop, a range of co-operative and interactive skills as well as their speaking and listening skills. All activities have a common format as follows:

Purpose – what the particular activity is aiming to achieve

Preparation – any helpful prior work the teacher or class needs to have done

Procedure – a sequence of steps to be taken or the main stages in the activity

Extension/Variation – possible alternatives or follow-up work that can be done.

Whilst using only one or two of these activities in isolation will not really develop more creative 'futures thinking', neither is it necessary to use all of them. Ideally you will make your own selection from each chapter. In this way activities can be used to support each other and pupils become increasingly conversant with futures ideas. You can adapt both the process and content of these activities to suit your particular needs.

The activities in this chapter introduce children to the idea of thinking about the future and to ways of doing this. They can be used to 'warm up' the imagination; to help pupils explore what they, and others, think and feel about the future. This relates both to their personal lives and to the wider world. All the activities start in the 'here and now' with pupils' everyday concerns.

> *"A child is a person who is going to carry on what you have started... He will assume control of your cities, states and nations... all your books are going to be judged, praised or condemned by him... the fate of humanity is in his hands."*

Source: Abraham Lincoln

When we teach children about the wider world we need, first of all, to find out what they know, or think they know, and what their perceptions of other people and countries are. Generally we find a mix of information drawn from parents, peers, the media, books and previous work in school. We also always find misperceptions and stereotypes to do with, for example, gender and nationality. The same applies when we study time.

Children will probably have relatively limited or fixed ideas about the future based on stereotypical views of how things will change. These need to be brought out into the open, to be shared, discussed and subjected to critical reflection. We should not be surprised, for example, if their ideas about the future are initially of the 'spaceships and robots' variety. One of the main purposes of this book is to help pupils move beyond such perceptions.

Source: Reproduced with permission. Judge Dredd is © Fleetway Editions Ltd. 1993

In *'Questions about the future'* pupils identify issues that interest them and the class and then carry out their own research to arrive at some answers to their questions. This enables the teacher to ascertain the pupils' concerns, to highlight the future as a subject worthy of study, and to reveal that there are no 'right' answers about the future.

In *'Continuity and change'* children are encouraged to become more aware of continuity and change in their lives and the world around them. What changes? What stays the same? What changes are part of the natural cycle of birth, growth, maturity, decline and death? What changes as a result of human activity and who has the power to make changes on behalf of others?

'Images of the future' explores the images that pupils have of the future. Are they optimistic or pessimistic? They will certainly be influenced by explicit, or more often implicit, images of the future from the media.

Pupils' images, like their questions, provide the initial raw material and starting points for more in-depth explorations.

'Exploring consequences' introduces the idea of futures wheels, a graphic method of mapping the consequences of decisions and choices. This activity helps pupils begin to develop foresight and to realise that all actions in the present, both their own and those of others, will have consequences in future time. It stresses the need to ascertain possibly unforeseen and undesirable consequences.

In *'The 200-year present'* the relationships between past, present and future can be examined. Some members of the community will have been born 100 years ago and some born today will live to be 100. What are the links between generations? What has been passed on between them? What would we like to pass on?

Finally, in *'Probable futures'*, children use timelines to explore how they *expect* the future to be. This can be for themselves, their community and for the wider world. They explore their own, and other peoples', expectations for the future. How might such futures affect their lives? Are these futures ones they would look forward to?

Taken together these activities begin to provide pupils with a conceptual framework for thinking about the future: in relation to themselves, society and the wider world.

QUESTIONS ABOUT THE FUTURE

Purpose

To encourage children to formulate their own questions about the future and to identify the particular interests of the class.

Preparation

Collect and make available books which deal with different aspects of the future. These may be about particular issues, for example the environment. NB Many topic books tend to give somewhat limited images of the future.

Children's questions about the future

Year 3/4 (eight to nine year olds), Blackbrook School, Taunton

- Will I still be laughing when I'm 50?
- Will we find out about Pluto?
- Will our friends be the same?
- What will our mums and dads look like?
- Will there be a war soon?
- How many more animals will be extinct?
- Will the jungles be destroyed?
- Will cars still have leaded petrol?
- Will pollution stop divers going under the sea?
- Will people still use pencils?
- Will they invent irons to run off solar heat?

Source: Cathie Holden

Year 3/4 (eight to nine year olds), Camp JMI School, St Albans

- Will there be an end to war?
- Will we stop polluting the environment?
- What is it going to be like at secondary school?
- Will we get a good education?
- What sort of jobs will we get?
- Will my family be happy?
- Is there life after death?
- Will we visit another country?
- Will there be a judgement day?
- Will there be equal opportunity and fairness in the world?

Source: Lisa Webb

Year 7/8 (12-13 year olds), State Middle School Basile, Naples

- Will we have the mafia in Giugliano?
- Will schools be better organised?
- What will we do when we're grown up?
- Will people waste the Earth's resources?
- What will we find after death?
- Will boys and girls have the same rights?
- How will the end of the world happen?
- Will there be another war?
- Will there be rich and poor people?

Source: Annamarie de Chiara

Procedure

- Each child writes down individually five questions she or he would like to ask about the future. They may be personal, about school, the local community, or events in the wider world.
- Children then work in groups of five or six to put similar questions together and then rank them by popularity. Each group identifies their 'top 10' questions.
- Alternatively the aim can be to produce a class 'top 10' questions. Three examples of this are shown opposite (left). They are a good illustration of pupils' current concerns and interests.

Extension

- It is often interesting to identify questions on the basis of gender. You can set up single sex groups during the stage of identifying and raising questions. Do the concerns of boys and girls or of different ethnic groups differ and if so how? Do they go about finding out answers in different ways?
- A more closed form of question could relate to specific subjects, for example the future of the school, the local neighbourhood, environmental issues.

by children of the World
with an introduction by
Boutros Boutros-Ghali
Secretary-General
United Nations

Source: Reproduced with the kind permission of Peace Child International and Kingfisher Books.

CONTINUITY AND CHANGE

Purpose

To help children become more aware of continuity and change in their own lives and in the wider world.

Preparation

Pupils will need copies of the two tables in Resource 4.1, 'Things that are changing' and 'Things that stay the same', and copies of the three photographs in Resource 4.2.

Procedure

- Begin with a class brainstorm to obtain as many responses as possible to the question: What do you think of when you hear the word 'change'? Even if the class is familiar with the technique of brainstorming, remind pupils of the three rules: i) all responses should be stated as briefly as possible; ii) all offerings are valid; and iii) no comments are made about other peoples' contributions.
- When enough varied examples of change have been written up on the board or overhead projector, focus discussion on questions such as: How common is change? What different sorts of change are there? How does change occur? NB A useful point to bring out is the distinction between natural change, for example the rhythm of the seasons or growing older, and change brought about as the result of human activity, for example moving house or building a new road. What kinds of change do pupils feel are most important in their own lives?
- Pupils then individually record some of the changes that they feel are most important at different scales using Resource 4.1, 'Things that are changing'.
- The next step is to work in small groups to discuss and agree, if possible, whether different changes are for the 'better' or 'worse' in their effects on people or the environment. Mark beneficial changes with a '✓', harmful changes with a 'x' and changes they're not sure about, or which they think are neither beneficial nor harmful with a '?'.

● Several points may need following up, for example that one person's '✓' is another person's 'x', and that change is all around us. Are there any relationships between the changes at different scales?

● Go through the same sequence, again using Resource 4.1 but this time looking at things that stay the same. Pupils individually record some of the things that they feel stay the same at different scales.

● Are different sorts of continuity beneficial or harmful? What conclusions do they come to about continuity?

● Finally, are there any particular people, or groups of people, in society which appear to be particularly responsible for change or continuity and who might they be? Children may identify adults (in relation to children), men (in relation to women), business (in relation to consumers), politicians, scientists, etc.

Extension

● One obvious simplification is to complete only one column at a time in the tables. Another way of looking at the connections between personal, local and global is to draw a more free-flowing web. Connections between things are rarely linear.

● The photographs in Resource 4.2 can provide starting points for discussion. Which illustrate continuity and which change. Why?

● Pupils can also look at different groups in society to see if, and how, their lives are changing or staying the same. For example, 'What is changing for women/what staying the same?'

Things that are changing

In my life	Locally	In Britain	In the world
My Bisical	TESCO	Spice Girls Baby scary victora	Diana Died
My fence	VIDOW	Weather	Water on moon
My Garden	Food and Drink Peper	Peopel	Elton Jhon Sr
My Home	Shop it	flowers	floods save me Help
My family	Hotel	Animals	tornadow Help

Source: Katie, aged eight

Resource 4.1

Things that are changing			
In my life	Locally	In Britain	In the world

Things that stay the same			
In my life	Locally	In Britain	In the world

Resource 4.2

© T Bertrand/Robert Harding

© Brian E Rybolt/Impact

© Nigel Francis/Robert Harding

A project on exploring change at St Scholastica's Roman Catholic School, London E5

Because Year 6 [11 year olds) was due to make the important change in their own lives of transferring to secondary school, change was the theme on which their science and humanities work was based for the term.

Our work began with a class brainstorm of all the things that the students perceive to be changing in the world around them. The brainstorm was then classified into changes that were personal, those which had local effect, those which affected the whole of this country, and those which had worldwide impact. The issues raised reflected concern felt by the students for the environment, human rights and personal fulfilment. After discussion, the students wrote in pairs to organisations concerned with such issues, asking specifically for information about how they work for change. The returned replies were kept for later use.

We moved on to investigate how the immediate area around the school has changed and went out with an OS map to colour code the ways in which land has been used in the area. These maps were then compared to 100 year old maps of the same area and differences noted. Meanwhile, in smaller groups, we went out with one of the staff from the Hackney Urban Studies Centre to survey types of local housing which ranged from 100 year old family houses and 1930s low rise flats, to tower blocks built in the 1960s and newly built terraces. After the fieldwork, we discussed the ways in which housing has changed in the area and used the Hackney Society book of oral history accounts, "The Island", to build on the information gained and develop a picture of the overall changes locally. We continued this by inviting two local people who had lived in the neighbourhood for a long time to come and be interviewed, which proved very interesting.

Following a public consultation about developments at Dalston Cross shopping centre, we asked Hackney Planning Department if we could borrow the exhibition which had been there. The students examined the displays and considered the options presented for improving the shopping facilities, access and safety for disabled people and the transport network of the area. An officer from the Planning Department was invited to the class to answer questions and explain the proposals further, as well as to clarify the role of planners in bringing about changes in the environment.

It was now time to think about the future and we gave out all the replies from organisations written to earlier in the project. From the leaflets and posters the students were asked to find out when the group was set up and by whom, why it was set up, whether young people could join it, what sort of future it is working for, and how successful it claimed to be. Following this the students worked in pairs to make their own timelines, showing first the changes in their own lives and lifetimes, and then making three separate pictures of the future: the future they would like to see; the future they would not like to see; and the future they expected to see.

The overwhelming concern expressed in the timelines was to do with environmental problems of pollution and global warming, reflecting the emphasis given to these issues by the media. Racism figured significantly in the 'futures we would not like to see', and there were many statements about education as the most significant way of both realising personal ambitions and of achieving justice and equality on a worldwide scale. Faith in inventions that might solve problems, eg solar powered vehicles, cropped up frequently, particularly in the 'expected future' lines. The timelines were discussed individually with each student as they were being produced and the main environmental concerns were raised with the whole class as far as time allowed.

To bring together all the strands of the term's work, we held a debate where each group of students chose to represent an organisation working for change and bidding for a mythical £1 million to carry out their work. Each group outlined the purposes of 'their' organisation and explained how they would be able to use more money to extend their aims or acquire something to increase their achievements. At the end of the debate the class voted overwhelmingly for giving the money to improve recycling facilities in this country, possibly reflecting their feelings expressed throughout the term's work that many environmental issues are too problematic to handle without considerable change in the ways economies are organised.

Source: Prue Poulton, Hackney Environmental Education Project

IMAGES OF THE FUTURE

Purpose

To discover what images of the future children already have and to explore where they come from.

Preparation

You will need paper and paints, coloured pens or other drawing materials.

Procedure

- Discuss with pupils ways in which they use their imagination to visualise things, for example to remember things that have happened in the past or to imagine a place they've never been to.
- Similarly it is possible to imagine what life might be like in the future, in the local community, in the UK, or in the world.
- Ask pupils to relax and close their eyes. Appropriate music can be played to aid this process. Tell them that they are going on a journey into the future, to the world in 2050. How old will they be then and what do they imagine the world will look like? Point out that this is not an exercise in 'prediction', neither are there any 'right' answers.
- Pupils should note what 'picture' of the future first comes to mind and concentrate upon this.
- They then individually draw or paint this image, without initially talking to anyone else.
- Then in pairs or small groups they describe their pictures to each other. Encourage them just to listen carefully and not to comment or criticise. Questions can be asked for clarification.
- Can these images be categorised in any way? For example, optimistic or pessimistic; personal, local or global; or by subject matter. Do images differ according to race or gender? Have any key areas of life been missed out?
  NB This activity may well result in stereotyped images of the future, often of the 'spaceships and robots' variety. This is to be expected and highlights what then has to be worked with.

- Group discussion can then focus on the sources of such images. Where do they come from? Is it parental/adult opinion, popular comics, particular TV programmes, newspapers, events in the news, advertisements, books?
- Which sources of information have been most influential? Make a list to show which seem to be the most important. Make the point that the views we have of the future are often very selective and influenced by the media.

Extension

- Over a period of a week pupils scan comics, magazines, papers and adverts for any references to the future. These are collected and displayed.
- What views of the future do these sources project? How similar or different are they to the children's original images? Who created these images and what for? Who benefits from them? Are these futures ones that we would like to come about or not?
- One point to be made in conclusion is that particular interest groups such as the media, business, or politicians, often play on people's hopes and fears for the future.

Images of the future

The children first closed their eyes while I encouraged them to think about the future. They then proceeded according to the suggested steps. I was working with a small mixed ability group of eight children, four boys and four girls, aged 10 and 11. They drew underwater scenes depicting humans living there; a very peaceful scene of people picking apples; returning to their mother's home in Malta; volcano-proof houses on stilts; flying cars; aliens invading.

Five pictures were optimistic and two pessimistic in their views of the future. There was a distinct difference according to gender, easily recognised by the children. The girls' images were peaceful scenes of animals and nature. The boys' images related to metal, killing, flying, volcanoes and houses. Subsequently they felt they had left out jobs, families, school, themselves and the ozone layer. The main influence regarding images of the future was films, such as "Back to the future", "The Terminator" and "Turtles". Television, books, family events and parents were also mentioned as sources of information – but not teachers!

Source: Amber Carroll, St Teresa's RC Primary School, Borehamwood, Hertfordshire

---

EXPLORING CONSEQUENCES

Purpose

To help children explore the wide-ranging consequences that can follow from a particular decision, trend or event in the present.

Preparation

You will need sheets of A3 paper and a variety of coloured pens; a copy of Resource 4.3 for each group of pupils. Resource 4.4 might be useful for the extension activity.

Procedure

- Children are given Resource 4.3, an example of a consequence wheel completed by older pupils.
- They then work in small groups to decide what issue they wish to explore. This might be the effect of banning cigarette advertisements, or of not making racist remarks in the playground, for example.
- The issue is written in the centre of the sheet of paper and a series of concentric circles drawn lightly around this point. The first question is 'What are the immediate consequences?' The group discusses what they think these might be and briefly write them round the first circle. This shows they are the first consequence to arise from this action or issue, for example 'meals prepared faster' in Resource 4.3.

- Next pupils discuss what consequences may follow on from the first ones. Such 'second order' consequences are written in the next ring.
- Succeeding third and fourth order consequences can be explored and marked in a similar fashion. It is not necessary to track every consequence as far as it will go!
- The end result is a wheel showing a range of possible consequences likely to flow from a particular decision. Different relationships may be observed between different areas. In particular, discussion is likely to focus around whether 'B' does actually follow 'A'.

Extension

- It is important that pupils should explore the difference between intended and unintended consequences of particular technological innovations, such as increased car ownership (see Resource 4.4), genetic engineering or genetically modified foods.

Resource 4.3

A consequences wheel

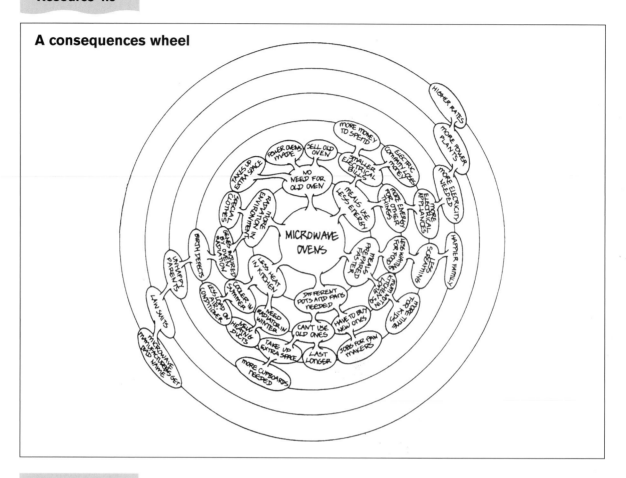

Resource 4.4

DRIVING YOU CRAZY

More than 100,000 cars are now produced a day, 50 million every year with numbers inexorably rising. The roads are swimming in more blood than is shed in modern battle: 250,000 people were killed last year by motor vehicles and 10 million injured.

Twenty years ago there were 100 million cars and trucks in use. Last year it was 500 million... New figures suggest that a fifth of our cities' space is now devoted to cars; an average American or European spends up to a quarter of his waking life on the road or gathering the money to be driving; the internal combustion engine drives oil wars and terrible pollution. And if that weren't enough, the scientists believe the car will soon tip us into global warming... [but] research shows people are "deeply concerned" about what cars do until they actually come to buy one.

The application of new technology clearly is causing problems as well as solving them. For though one may feel that on balance the rapid advance of technology is a blessing, there clearly are enormous costs. And if all the costs were properly weighted and a judicious decision made, society might reject much new technology that seems at first glance to offer only benefits... We can never do just one thing. Every action radiates forward in time and outward in space, affecting everything everywhere.

Source: John Vidal. © The Guardian, 18 October 1991

Source: Edward Cornish. Reproduced with permission of The Futurist, World Future Society, Bethesda, Maryland, USA

THE 200-YEAR PRESENT

Purpose

To help children explore relationships between past, present and future and to develop a sense of chronology.

Preparation

Some previous activities on thinking about the future would be helpful. You will need copies of Resources 4.5 and 4.6 for each child.

Procedure

- Introduce the class to Elise Boulding's idea of the extended 200-year present (see Resource 4.5). The class is going to explore its own such present through talking to parents and grandparents, or other older relations and neighbours, and anticipating the lives of their own future children and grandchildren.
- It is useful to have pictures or illustrations that help children actually see these relationships. One example is show in Resource 4.6. Alternatively this could take the form of five human figures on a 200-year timeline. From left to right are: grandparent – parent – the pupil – the pupil's grown-up child – the pupil's grown-up grandchild.
- An actual or approximate date of birth can be put under each figure. NB The average interval between the birth of successive generations is supposed to be 30/33 years.
- These relationships can then be explored in a variety of ways. For example, children could:
  - Interview parents, relations or other adults about what life was like when they were children. How was it different, how the same?
  - Interview a grandparent or older relative/neighbour about what their childhood was like. How was it different/the same to their own/their parent's childhood?
  - Bring items such as old photographs, toys or birth certificates into school to stimulate the imagination.
  - Find out about the most important events in their parents' and grandparents' (or others') lives. What were the biggest changes seen by each generation? A collage can be made to illustrate these changes.
  - Find out if any special stories or objects have been passed down in their families?
- This sort of activity may well be familiar to pupils from work in history. What makes it different is the second half of the sequence, looking to the future, which is essential.
  - How do children think the world might be different when they are a pensioner? When will this be?
  - What objects, qualities, wishes would they like to pass on to their children and grandchildren?
  - What future events do they hope will happen in the lifetime of their children and grandchildren?
  - Pupils could write a letter to one of their future grandchildren telling them: i) what their own life is like and ii) in what ways they hope their world will be better than today.
  - In how many different ways are these generations related? What do they pass on to each other? Pupils may initially think of objects being handed down, but this can also apply to qualities or physical appearance.
  - Do we have a responsibility to help future generations, for example our children and grandchildren? What might we do *now* that they would be grateful for in the future?
- While it may be easier to explore the last 100 years, the next 100 equally demand our attention. We need to develop pupils' skills of anticipation; the understanding that decisions made now have effects far into the future; that we have a responsibility to future generations.

Extension

- The latter part of this activity can be directly linked with 'Rights of future generations' (see pages 45–47).
- Older pupils might like to read a book such as Alison Utley's *The Country Child*, which graphically illustrates life at the beginning of our extended present.

Resource 4.5

The extended present

...a medium range of time, which is neither too long or too short for immediate comprehension, and which has an organic quality that gives it relevance for the present moment. This medium range is the 200-year present. That present begins 100 years ago today, on the day of birth of those among us who are centenarians. Its other boundary is the 100th birthday of the babies born today. This present is a continuously moving moment, always reaching out 100 years in either direction from the day we are in. We are linked with both boundaries of this moment by the people among us whose life began or will end at one of those boundaries, five generations each way in time. It is our space, one that we can move around in directly in our own lives and indirectly by touching the lives of the young and old around us.

Source: Elise Boulding (1988) *Building a Global Civic Culture: Education for an Interdependent World*, New York: Teachers College Press

Resource 4.6

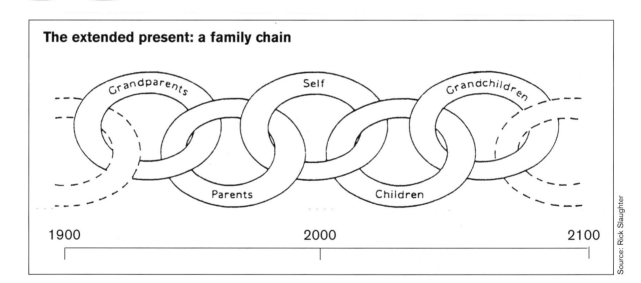

The extended present: a family chain

Grandparents — Self — Grandchildren

Parents — Children

1900   2000   2100

Source: Rick Slaughter

PROBABLE FUTURES

Purpose

For children to explore how they expect the future to be, both in their own lives and in society more widely.

Preparation

Some knowledge of events now happening in the world is useful. It is also useful to have discussed some important events that have occurred locally and globally during the children's lifetime. Sheets of A3 paper and a variety of coloured pens are needed.

Procedure

● Introduce the idea of a timeline, that is setting out actual and/or likely events along a specific timescale. The line should start with the child's year of birth and then be marked off in 10 year intervals for 50 years ahead.

● Pupils then write on their line what they feel have been the most important personal events in their lives so far.

- The main task is for pupils to work in pairs to each consider what events they feel are *likely* to happen to them in their lives. (NB they are not dealing here with what they *hope* will come about. This is a later activity.) This should be preceded by some class or small group discussion. Key events are likely to be changing school, leaving school, getting a job, living with a partner, deciding whether to have children or not, changing jobs and so on. When do pupils think they will be 'grown up'? When will they be middle-aged? To what age do they expect to live? Do boys and girls have different expectations?

- Encourage pupils to illustrate the timeline in different ways. They are then shared and compared in small groups. What similarities and differences are there?

- Next pupils work in pairs to draw and complete a second timeline on probable events and trends in the wider world. The starting and finishing dates should be the same as before. What important national/global events have occurred in the children's lifetimes?

- Finally, what future events and trends do pupils consider will *probably* come about and when? What different ways of illustrating them can children think of? Completed timelines make an excellent wall display.

Extension

- An alternative for the wider world timeline is to let pupils go back as far as they wish in time. What are the 'important' events that they would mark on? An example of this is shown in the 'Global timeline' below.

- Is the class as a whole generally optimistic or pessimistic about the future? How did pupils decide whether something was likely or not? Who will benefit most from the probable future they have outlined? Would they like to live in it?

- The final step is to compare personal and global timelines. If the probable national/global events come about, how might they affect pupils' lives? How may pupils' personal lives and choices affect the wider world? Are there discrepancies between the two?

Global timeline by Eleanor, aged 7

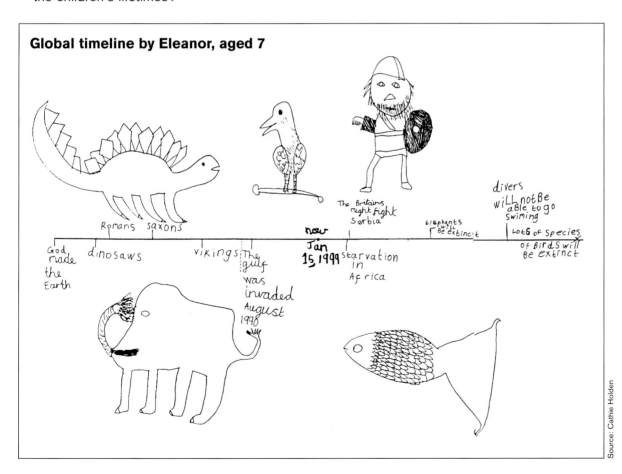

Source: Cathie Holden

INTRODUCTION

The activities in this chapter introduce children to ways of imagining or envisioning desirable futures. This is important because citizens of the 21st century need to be open to new experiences, new ideas and unfamiliar concepts. They will need to develop both their critical thinking skills and their creative imagination.

Since the future is not fixed or ultimately predictable, any number of alternative futures might seem possible. However, as a result of choices already made in the past our options are being continually reduced. Future generations therefore have no choice of a nuclear-free future. Even if nuclear weapons were to be outlawed and (after the accident at Chernobyl) power stations closed down, future generations will still need to store our radioactive waste safely for 250,000 years, that is for 8,000 generations.

Similarly, the continual loss of topsoil to farming and of innumerable plant and animal species, reduces the range of futures available to future generations. Choices made in the past are limiting our options now and in the future. It is vitally important, therefore, that we think not only about probable futures (how things are likely to be) but also about preferable futures (how we feel things *ought* to be). Being able to envision futures which are more life-enhancing than today, both personally and globally, is now a vital survival skill.

Many powerful groups in society also work to shape the future to their own ends. In the world as a whole, for example, six times as much public money is spent on weapons research as for research on health protection. This discrepancy will seriously affect people's health and thus their life-chances in the future. Different choices in the present would result in a quite different future.

Transnational corporations, for example, 'colonise' the future by shaping our desires and needs through marketing and advertising, whether the cars we drive, what we eat or the clothes we wear. At Christmas recently, just one business sold: enough tinsel to go round the M25 forty times (4,500 miles); enough Christmas tree lights to stretch between London and New York (3,500 miles); enough boxes of chocolates to equal the weight of seven jumbo

jets (2,500 tonnes); 11 million crackers and 250 million cards. [1] Such commercial forces clearly shape the future and say more about human greed than human need.

However, working together with others of like mind, whether in political parties, community organisations or pressure groups, can create all sorts of change, from better wages and working hours to the dissolution of national boundaries. People's images of the future do have a major influence on what they feel it worth working for in the present.

"Women are better adapted for the change from the industrial society to a new society... because women are not carriers of the values of the preceding industrial society. As they were not the builders of the future in the preceding society, they may become the builders of the future in a different society. As they were invisible in the industrial society, they may become visible and constructive in a post-industrial society."

Source: Elenora Masini (1987) 'Women as builders of the future', *Futures*, August.

Clarifying preferable futures can provide motivation in the present, whether to pass an exam, train for a particular job, or join a local action group. It is easiest to work towards the future we prefer if we have a clear picture of where we'd like to get to. Positive guiding images of the future are also more likely to facilitate change.

The activities in this chapter help children to identify their choices and preferences for the future. They encourage the development of imagination, intuition and creativity. They also draw attention to the needs of others and to the planet: they are about both rights and responsibilities. Taken together these activities help to answer the question: 'Where do we want to get to?', both in the local and global community.

Robin Richardson expressed this succinctly when he wrote:

> "A map without utopia on it, it has been said, is not worth consulting... Admittedly there are disadvantages of unreality and abstractions. But frequently it also clears and strengthens your mind if you venture to dream for a while, as concretely and as practically as possible, about the ideal situation to which all your current efforts are, you hope, directed." [2]

> "You must give birth to your images
> They are the future waiting to be born
> Fear not the strangeness you feel
> The future must enter into you long
> Before it happens."

Source: Rainer Maria Rilke

> "Where there is no vision the people perish."

Source: Proverbs 29:18

> "The only way to discover the limits of the possible is to go beyond them to the impossible."

Source: Arthur C Clarke

> "Be realistic, demand the impossible!"

Source: Student slogan 1968

> "Imagination is more important than knowledge."

Source: Albert Einstein

In 'My ideal place' pupils are given the opportunity to describe and share with others their favourite places, both real and imaginary. What do such places say about our values and priorities? This leads to consideration of the important notion of utopia and its role in encouraging visions of a better world.

In 'Preferable futures' the idea of timelines is used to help pupils map their preferred futures, both personal and global. Comparisons can be made with previous work on probable futures and attention drawn to discrepancies between the two. What changes are needed to turn the probable into the preferable?

In 'Rights of future generations' pupils are invited to consider the idea that each generation should inherit no less natural or human wealth than the one before. They explore both the notion of human rights and how they should extend over time as well as space.

'Goals for a better world' identifies five broad areas of concern and invites pupils to explore them in relation to both the local and global community. This helps to make the concept of preferable futures more specific and goal-orientated.

In 'Letters to the future' pupils are given the opportunity to write to their descendants and describe their hopes for them in the future. They also have the opportunity to 'listen' to what future generations might want to say to them.

The 'Council of All Beings' provides an opportunity for pupils to develop compassion for other life-forms and, through drama and role-play, to explore some of the difficulties that humans create for them.

Taken together these activities encourage the process of creative visualisation of desirable futures, a vital element in the realisation of personal, social and political change.

MY IDEAL PLACE

Purpose

To encourage use of the creative imagination and to introduce children to the concept of utopia.

Preparation

A collection of stimulus pictures, photographs and music is helpful. You will need copies of Resources 5.1 and 5.2 for each child.

Procedure

● Remind the class that everyone has some picture of their ideal place. It may be somewhere particular they like to visit or it may be in their imagination.
● What are some of the children's *real* ideal places and what do they like doing there? Is it a particular shop, a place to meet friends, somewhere they've been on holiday? They can write about this place, make a sketch and draw a map of it.
● In small groups pupils take it in turns to describe their ideal place. What is it that makes it so special? How often do they go there? What do they do there? Do they go with others?

• Next pupils think about their *imaginary* ideal place. These can be equally as important as real places. They can be visited in the imagination whenever one wants. A short written description or drawing should be made and shared. What are the similarities and difference between pupils' real and imaginary ideal places? Do they vary depending on gender?

• A wall display or scrapbook can be made out of these combined descriptions.

MAGIC SPOT.

At my magic spot I was in a different world. My magic spot was under a tree and behind a hill.Rain ran down it's trunk and there was lots of lichen and moss on it,it was better then any other tree I had seen before so I rushed to it. It was comfy. I found a worm and a beetle. I dug a hole and put the worm in it.At my magic spot I thought about nature and trees,plants,every thing.I thought it was beautiful.

Source: Beech Hill Primary School, Wigan

• Explain that ideal societies are often called utopias, a word made up by Thomas More. It is a pun on the Greek words for 'good place' and 'no place'. He used it as the title of a story he wrote in 1516 in which he described his ideal society. The term utopia is thus also used to mean a vision of a better world. Since Thomas More's time many people have written about their utopias and sometimes even tried to set them up. Envisioning our utopias allows us to explore different notions of the ideal society and thus to clarify our hopes for a better future. As William Morris wrote 100 years ago: "I want to tell you what it is I desire of the Society of the Future, just as if I were going to be reborn into it."

• Pupils read the brief description of *News from Nowhere* (Resource 5.1) written by William Morris in the 1890s and the description of Sheffield as it might be in the year 2040 (Resource 5.2). This sort of utopia is sometimes called an 'ecotopia' because it is particularly concerned about ecological issues. They then answer the following questions: In what ways is life in this community of 2040 different from today? In particular, think about use of

technology, neighbourhood facilities, transport and communications, work and politics. What are the advantages of the sort of society described here?

• Pupils work in small groups to plan their own ideal community or society. How would people live? How would they relate to each other? How would education and work be organised? How would the needs of different groups, such as the young, old, disabled, or women, be met? Who would make the decisions in the community?

• What changes need to be made in society today to achieve such a utopia? How many of these changes are already visible today? What groups are already working to bring about such changes?

"You and I can each think of a place, or more likely a succession of places, that matter most especially to us. Because of their beauty or some moment... we associate with them, or because we divine in them some power to which we may have access, we visit them often in our imaginations. If anything, these personal places grow more dear to us as the years pass. In our minds they exist outside time and we see them with a kind of quickened eye and raised consciousness."

Source: K Crossley-Holland (1989) *The Stones Remain: Megalithic Sites of Britain*, Rider,1989

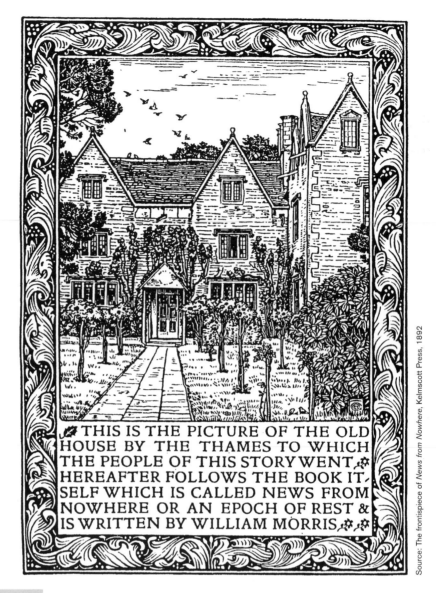

THIS IS THE PICTURE OF THE OLD HOUSE BY THE THAMES TO WHICH THE PEOPLE OF THIS STORY WENT. HEREAFTER FOLLOWS THE BOOK IT. SELF WHICH IS CALLED NEWS FROM NOWHERE OR AN EPOCH OF REST & IS WRITTEN BY WILLIAM MORRIS.

Source: The frontispiece of *News from Nowhere*, Kelmscott Press, 1892

Resource 5.1

William Morris and utopia

Over 100 years ago William Morris looked at the England he lived in and saw widespread poverty, violence and greed. This lead him to think about the society he would like to live in and so he wrote a famous story called *News from Nowhere*. (What did the Greek word utopia mean?) In this he describes how he fell asleep one night and awoke to find himself a visitor in the 21st century. Here he finds the London he knows has totally changed. Everything ugly has been removed and people live freely and happily together, with everyone having enough for their needs. The dirty factories of Victorian England have disappeared; so too has the use of money and the need for centralised government. Indeed he learns that the Houses of Parliament are used for storing manure from the local farms! As he is shown round this utopian future society, he realises that all aspects of life have changed, from industry and work to leisure and education. He thus paints a vivid picture of the world he would like to see, of the ideal society he hopes will come to exist in the future.

A day in Sheffield 2040

It is June 2040 and Jane Pearson wakes early with the sun shining down on the family house in East End Park, Sheffield. The solar collector on the roof has warmed the water for Jane's shower and, by the time she has dressed and gone downstairs, husband Tom is giving Jake his breakfast. Before sitting down with them, Jane takes some old newspapers and bottles out to the bins in the backyard. There are different bins for paper, glass, plastic, metals and organic waste, and their contents will be collected by the District Recycling Centre that afternoon.

Jane, Jake and Tom tuck into their breakfast of cereals and fresh fruit from the neighbourhood orchards. A lot of food is now grown in the valley and Tom spends some of his time helping at the local fish farm. It has taken a long time to reclaim the polluted soils and this could not have been done without the use of compost from the recycling centre and sewage works. Better soils have made it easier to grow crops and to establish green corridors through the valley where many wild plants and animals now live. These help clean the air and water, and keep everyone in touch with the natural world.

Tom leaves the house to go to the bus stop with Jake in the child's seat on the back of his bike. Trams were reintroduced into Sheffield in 1988 and now provide fast, clean free public transport through the city. Most people live near enough to work to walk or cycle, but Tom's father is disabled and needs the tram to get him to the community centre where he helps look after young children like Jake.

Most of the small businesses in the valley are owned by their workers. They all have a say in what is made and how it is produced and can be elected to be supervisors or managers. Workers are usually on flexi-time, allowed to work no more than 30 hours each week and given time off for re-training. Tom is only 35, but has already had three jobs and is now looking forward to leaving the co-op to teach design and technology in the neighbourhood school.

Jane is already involved with East End Park School. A small group of students have come round during the day to help her repair some bikes. Cycle repair, solar collector installation and greenhouse construction are all now part of the GCSE Practical Technology examination which the members of the group will be taking. They include not only teenagers but also adults who join school classes as one way of meeting their educational and training needs.

The Pearsons are going to eat in the community café that evening so there is no need to do food shopping or hurry home. The community café – like the community laundry – is a way of sharing domestic work and saving energy. Some people work in them for wages which are set by the community meeting, but most people work in them to obtain services at a cheaper rate and to meet their neighbours. This evening all the talk over dinner is about the community meeting at eight o'clock.

The people of East End Park have regular community meetings with members of their neighbourhood council which then sends representatives to the Lower Don Valley Council. All people over 16 who live in East End Park are eligible to sit on the neighbourhood council and its membership is decided by a computer which selects 20 names at random every four years. This method of selecting councillors means that most people take an interest in local affairs, and neighbourhood meetings are generally crowded and lively.

Tonight's meeting is about the future of the huge indoor shopping centre built near the M1 motorway in the 1990s. Neighbourhoods, cities and regions are now much more self-sufficient. People produce more of what they need locally and do not have to travel far to shop. They are also less interested in consumer goods than people were 50 years ago. The huge spaces set aside for shopping and car parking are now becoming derelict and the City Council has asked neighbourhoods to consider new uses for the land.

The suggestions put forward at the meeting include a hospital specialising in acupuncture, a National Museum of the Consumer Age, a freight marshalling yard for British Rail, a botanical garden, and housing for overseas students. Jane is elected to a group of councillors who will consider the proposals in more detail and bring ideas back to the next meeting.

Source: Adapted from John Huckle (1990) *Environment and Democracy*, WWF-UK

PREFERABLE FUTURES

Purpose

For children to explore how they would like the future to be, both in their own lives and in the wider world.

Preparation

The activity on 'Probable futures' (pages 36–37) should have been carried out. Sheets of A3 paper and a variety of coloured pens are needed. An example of a timeline combining probable and preferable futures would be useful – see Resource 5.3.

Procedure

- Remind the class of the work previously done on probable futures using timelines.
- The same process is used as before but this time to chart events that pupils *hope* will occur in their lives. This is initially done in relation to pupils' own lives. (See 'Variation' for an alternative way of doing this.)
- The timeline can be drawn and illustrated in any lively way which helps to illustrate the main events. Children then share and compare them in pairs or small groups. It is important to stress that hopes should be respected, not criticised.
- How do these preferable timelines compare with the previously drawn probable ones? How are they different? Are there particular areas of life where the differences are most marked? What would need to happen for the probable timeline to be more like the preferable one?
- Next pupils work in pairs to draw a second timeline marking preferable trends and events in the wider world. What would the future look like if pupils' hopes for the planet were realised? When do they hope particular things might come about?

- Remind the class of how dramatically things can change in a short period of time, whether the end of the British Empire over a 20 year period, or the collapse of communism and the former USSR in the space of a few years.
- When completed these global timelines should be displayed for the class to examine and compare. Children can make brief presentations and answer questions about their views. This is also a time for sharing and respecting pupils' hopes and visions.
- What similarities are there between these preferred global futures? Can the class arrive at a composite picture of their preferred future? Who would benefit most from this future? Will anyone lose?
- What events and trends happening in the world at present will support their hoped for changes? What can they themselves do to help such changes come about?
- A final step is to compare personal and global timelines. If the preferable global events come about, how would they affect pupils' lives? If there are discrepancies between the personal and global timelines, what needs to happen for them to become more in tune with each other?

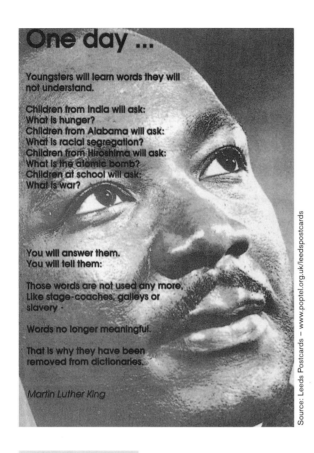

One day ...

Youngsters will learn words they will not understand.

Children from India will ask:
What is hunger?
Children from Alabama will ask:
What is racial segregation?
Children from Hiroshima will ask:
What is the atomic bomb?
Children at school will ask:
What is war?

You will answer them.
You will tell them:

Those words are not used any more,
Like stage-coaches, galleys or slavery ·

Words no longer meaningful.

That is why they have been removed from dictionaries.

Martin Luther King

Source: Leeds Postcards – www.poptel.org.uk/leedspostcards

Variation

● The most common variation for this activity is to combine both probable and preferable timelines as shown in Resource 5.3. The advantage of this is that the differences between probable and preferable futures are immediately visible. Global probable futures often tend to be pessimistic. By drawing both lines together fears are immediately offset by hopes. The actual gap between the two lines represents the area where changes need to occur. What is happening in the local community that related to the preferable timeline?

RIGHTS OF FUTURE GENERATIONS

Purpose

To help children understand that future generations will have needs and therefore rights similar to their own.

Resource 5.3

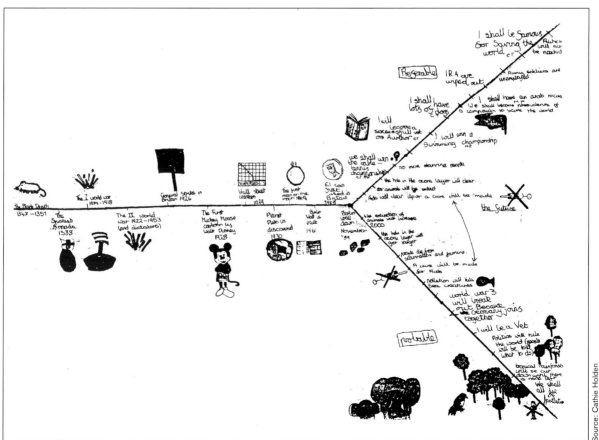

Source: Cathie Holden

Preparation

It will help if pupils have previously worked through activities such as 'The 200-year present' (pages 35–36) and 'Preferable futures' (pages 44–45). Some previous work on human rights would be useful. Pupils will need copies of Resources 5.4 and 5.5; alternatively, 5.4 could be copied onto a flipchart or chalkboard.

Procedure

- Whilst we cannot be sure what life will be like for people living, say, 50 years from now, there will be a range of basic things that they will need in order to enjoy a good quality of life. Reference can be made to the 200-year present to establish that we are talking about the needs and rights of the pupils' own children and grandchildren.
- First, brainstorm with the whole class 'Things we have inherited from previous generations'. This should include problems we have inherited as well as benefits. Examples might include the right to vote, better working conditions, better communications, as well as polluted water supplies, unemployment and the danger of AIDS. The results of the brainstorm should then be sorted into two columns headed 'Benefits' and 'Problems'. Is it easy to decide which is which?
- Secondly discussion should focus on how we, in the present, are already affecting the lives of future generations. This could also be done as a brainstorm. It should again include both positive and negative impacts.
- Thirdly, pupils work in groups to consider what needs and therefore what rights future generations should have. This needs to begin with a consideration of the proposal set out in Resource 5.4. It is based on work done by economists interested in sustainable development. [3]
- Pupils may need some initial prompting to grasp the broad definition of wealth intended here, namely homes, shops, businesses, industries, as well as money.

- What is meant by natural wealth? Here pupils might come up with mineral resources; clean air and water; a diverse range of species (animal and plant); good soil for farming; clean beaches; protected countryside and so on.
- What is happening at present that might mean the next generation inherits less of any of these than we have? What are people doing to make sure that the next generation *does* inherit as much as we did? The work of organisations such as Friends of the Earth, Amnesty International and WWF could be looked at here.
- The class then draw up their own 'Charter for Future Generations'. This can be compared with the example shown in Resource 5.5 and also with the UN Declaration of the Rights of the Child.

Variation

- On a timeline covering the last 100 years, pupils indicate the achievements made in their parents' and grandparents' lifetimes from which they now benefit.

international conference responsibilities towards future generations and their environment

valletta malta

27-29 april 1992

Resource 5.4

The rights of future generations

The argument is that to be fair each generation should inherit no less 'wealth', natural and person-made, than we (the present generation) have inherited. So the next generation has a right to expect to inherit at least as much 'wealth' as we did. As long as each generation does this, no single generation has to worry about generations far into the future. Each generation 'looks after' the one that follows.

Resource 5.5

A Charter for Future Generations

The right to a good education

The right to a clean, litter free place

The right to healthy food

The right to love and care

The right to reproduce

The right to care for the environment

The right to medical attention

The right to be heard and to have a say

The right to have friends

The right to a secure and warm home

Source: Year 6 (11 year olds), St Thomas's C of E School, Ashton-in-Makerfield

GOALS FOR A BETTER WORLD

Purpose

To help children identify goals for a better world. To relate these to their everyday lives.

Preparation

It will help if pupils have already done work on 'Preferable futures' (pages 44–45). 'Rights of future generations' (pages 45–47) and 'My ideal place' (pages 40–43). You will need sufficient copies of Resource 5.6 for groups of children. Resource 5.7 is needed for the 'Variation'.

Procedure

● Resource 5.6 outlines five broad goals for a better world. In groups, pupils firstly discuss each goal in relation to their local community by taking each of the following questions in turn:
  1 Why is this an important goal for a better society?
  2 How would it make my community better to live in?
  3 What is already being done to achieve these goals and by whom?
  4 What might we want to do to help achieve each of these goals?

● Pupils collect newspaper cuttings and make a montage to illustrate action to work towards such goals on a global scale.

Variations

● It is also important to consider how these goals might be perceived differently depending on gender, race, age or class. Do boys and girls view them differently and, if so, how? Do other cultural groups interpret these goals differently?

● Ask pupils to look at Resource 5.7. How might the people living in the community shown interpret these goals?

Resource 5.6

Five goals for a better world

1 *Personal welfare*

Everyone should have the basic necessities of life such as food, clothes, shelter, health care and education. There should be a minimum level of welfare, below which no one drops.

2 *Freedom from violence*

No one should be subjected to violence, for example attacked or robbed, and also no one should suffer from violence – directly or indirectly – by living under an unjust political system.

3 *Justice for all*

What one 'has' should not depend on who one 'is' in society or where one lives. No one should be deprived of the necessities of life or human rights because of their gender, race, class, culture, group or geographical location.

4 *Environmental care*

The natural environment, on which all life depends, also needs to be properly looked after and protected. It includes care of air, water, soil, creatures and plants.

5 *Participating in decisions*

People should have a say in all the decisions that will affect their lives. It means they should have the right to participate in decisions made by others that will affect them.

Source: After Johan Galtung

Resource 5.7

Source: © Ron Giling/Still Pictures

LETTERS TO THE FUTURE

Purpose

To encourage a sense of responsibility towards future generations.

Preparation

Previous work on 'The 200-year present' (pages 35–36), 'Preferable futures' (pages 44–45), or 'Rights of future generations' (pages 45–47) will provide a good grounding for this activity. Copies of Resource 5.8 on page 50 are needed for the 'Variation'.

Procedure

- Explain to pupils that they have the opportunity to write a letter to their grandchildren. What might they want to say?
- This is best done as a co-operative task where children work in pairs to consider the following questions:
  1 Who are you going to write to?
  2 Where will they live?
  3 What are your hopes for them in the future?
  4 How do you think events today may affect their lives?
  5 What can you do to help them now?
- When completed, these letters to the future can be read out and displayed.

Variation

- Letters can also, of course, be written individually and simply be addressed to 'My grandchild'. They can then be put in a sealed envelope and marked 'Do not open until ...'.
- A display of items can be made by the class to show how they are making a conscious effort to work for a better future. A small display can also be sealed up for opening at a future specified date.
- Pupils could also imagine that they have received a letter from the future. Resource 5.8 is an example of what people alive 200 years from now might say. After reading this, or a simplified version, pupils could write their own account of what actually happened during 'The Abrupt Transformation'.

15th November.

These I would like to leave my grandchildren.

I would like to leave my grandchildren a peaceful world. I would like to leave my grandchildren a world with no hole in the ozone layer and with no testing on animals. I would like there to be no killings and no wars.
I would like there to be people who are not racist or sexist.

Chantal age 11

Source: Amber Carroll

COUNCIL OF ALL BEINGS

Purpose

To foster compassion for all living things and to develop awareness of the dangers other species face.

Preparation

Pupils could have done some previous work on endangered species. Paper, coloured pens or paints, and face paints are needed.

Procedure

- Outline to pupils in advance the key stages in preparing for the Council of All Beings. [4]
- Plenty of space is needed and children are invited to find a place to sit or stand.
- A tape can be played of natural sounds, for example the sea or wind, or animal sounds. Pupils can lie down if they wish.
- The task is for pupils to think about another creature that they would like to represent. This could be any animal, or even plant, which particularly catches their imagination.
- Having chosen the creature that they wish to represent at the Council, pupils carry out their own research into its habits and habitat, shape, colours, size and the dangers it may face.
- Pupils can practise moving like their chosen creature and trying out appropriate sounds. They consider how their creature would wish to appear at the coming gathering and what their particular message to the Council might be.
- As preparation for this, pupils work in small groups taking it in turns to share with each other: what I look like; how I move; what my special qualities are.

A Letter from 2200 AD

We are glad that your generation became so acutely and accurately aware of your gravest dangers and most foolish paths. As a result, your period of history is admired by historians and is called The Abrupt Transformation. Perhaps the word 'abrupt' strikes you as too dramatic because your deep-rooted changes were actually spread over a decade. A period of 3,650 days may not feel abrupt to the people alive at the time, but to us 200 years later it seems a remarkably swift, courageous and admirable transformation.

Your period has gone down in human history as the time when the people of Earth finally took vigorous and effective action to virtually eliminate warfare and population growth, and to shift to a long-term sustainable relationship with the environment. You thus eliminated human civilisation's worst risks; a rather stunning achievement in just 10 years.

In addition, of course, you did your share to build foundations for a highly positive future for generations that were not yet born, and you contributed to that positive future in several specific ways. We are one of those shadowy generations that you could imagine only dimly in your distant future. We are very real to ourselves, of course, and very much alive, but to you we were just a vague, remote fantasy, since you had no way of picturing any details about us. The highly positive state of human civilisation today is due in large part to the efforts, commitment, courage and sacrifices of your generation and the other seven generations between you and us. We owe our advanced culture and our well-being to all of those generations.

To you, though, who created and lived through The Abrupt Transformation, we send our particular gratitude. You made some very hard choices that had been labelled 'unrealistic' and even 'impossible' because they were going to be so difficult. But you did make these changes and sacrifices – because enough of you saw that the consequences of any other path would be even more difficult and unpleasant. The immediate costs of changing were enormous, but the costs of not changing would have been much worse. Thank you for your courage in facing reality and in taking vigorous action.

Source: From Allen Tough (1993) *Critical Questions About the Future*, London: Adamantine Press

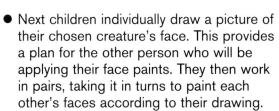

Source: Catherine Foxon

- Next children individually draw a picture of their chosen creature's face. This provides a plan for the other person who will be applying their face paints. They then work in pairs, taking it in turns to paint each other's faces according to their drawing.
- Once everyone's face is painted a period of quiet follows for children to identify more fully with their creature. Ask: What shape are you? What is your skin or surface like? How do you move? How big are you? What sounds, if any, do you make? What are you going to say about yourself at the Council?
- Then back in small groups of three or four, pupils practice speaking as their chosen species. What do they want to tell humans about themselves? This process helps deepen identification and acts as a rehearsal for the Council. How does it feel to be this creature? What are their particular strengths and qualities? Speaking should always be done in the first person.
- After these rehearsals everyone convenes in a large circle for the Council of All Beings. The teacher is the representative for human beings. There are three stages. First each creature takes it in turn, however briefly, to speak about themselves. Each says 'Who I am' and 'What my qualities are'. This may be quite simple, for example 'I am a butterfly. I float on the wind with delicate wings. I am a pretty colour.'

- Secondly, after everyone has done this, each creature is invited to say what is happening to them as a result of human actions. The butterfly might talk about the effect of herbicides and pesticides, or the disappearance of many of her kin.
- Finally, each creature names a particular gift they would like to give to humans to stop the current destruction of species. The butterfly, for example, might offer 'lightness of touch'.
- The Council can end in a variety of ways – music, laughter, animal calls, silence. As pupils leave to remove their face paints everyone can say "Thank you, butterfly" etc. There needs to be a clear transition back to the children's own identities and a letting go of the creature that they have been representing.
- Finally the group reconvenes in a circle to share their experiences. Initially children take it in turn to speak, with the others just listening. Then discussion can move towards what they might want to do as a result of what they've learnt.
- They may like to draw up a 'Charter for All Beings' such as the one shown on page 53. Information can be made available on what others are doing, for example groups such as WWF and Friends of the Earth.

The Council of All Beings

This activity really attracted me and I felt younger children (Year 4/nine year olds) could get a lot from it. Movement seemed the key into the activity as it would deepen their experience of being another life form. During a 45 minute PE lesson the children explored different ways of moving, individually and in groups, as they listened to a tape of bird and animal sounds before lying on the earth to decide what to be.

The second session lasted all morning and began with the class in groups of four or five speaking 'in role' and describing special qualities they each had. What did their creatures look like? Books were consulted and faces of their species were drawn, coloured and labelled. Drawing a 'plan' to use for face painting presented some children with a real challenge; others produced very detailed images and instructions.

Painting each other's faces absorbed and delighted the class, who worked with care to follow their partner's plans. This avoided the need for mirrors, required co-operation and respect, and helped move the activity along briskly. The classroom was full of shared laughter and each pair went to see themselves in the cloakroom mirrors when finished. Important!

Then we talked about the forthcoming Council of All Beings and what each species would say before going to the hall, where the tape used in the first session was playing. The class moved readily as their chosen creatures and were eager to begin the

Council. As representative of the human species, I welcomed all creatures to the Council – they flew, crawled and hopped into the circle. The excitement level was quite high. There were introductions, problems stated and acknowledged, and a short break to move about in role when some got restless. The woodpecker went off to peck the wall bars! This relieved the strain of sitting but did not break concentration levels at all. The Council re-convened to share the gifts they would like to send to humans. The activity ended with each creature being thanked. Each then left the circle, moving in role until reaching the door.

The Council created great empathy and the children wanted to do something. They decided humans

Source: The Peaceable Kingdom. Reproduced with Permission of Karin van Heerden

needed to know what they had found out. Next day, a meeting of species was called (extended language work) where some wrote in role about themselves and their experiences. A discussion that should have been taped followed – they had great commitment and understanding now. Many suggestions were put forward and the class decided on the six best ones for a Charter (a recent topic had involved Magna Carta). This was special: done on parchment and beautifully decorated with drawings of the creatures at the Council. Other classes were visited and the Charter was read out in Assembly before an 'official presentation' was made to humans.

A Charter
for the world
a message to humans
① Stop hunting and punish hunters.
② Stop buying animal skins and ivory.
③ Stop buying things tested on animals.
Stop and think what you are doing.
④ Be careful not to pollute seas and rivers.
⑤ Think of your children's future.

Choosing the Future

INTRODUCTION

Imagining the future

"The future is, and must always remain, in a fundamental sense, unknowable. The best that futures research can do is to explore possible alternative futures. Since we are confronted with such uncertainty about the future, it would be the height of folly to take a single, simplistic view of it, and to claim that we can predict the future. Rather we should limit our claims to exploring multiple, possible futures. For this reason our best hope is to try and bracket the future by means of a set of scenarios, each dealing with possible alternatives." [1]

Scenarios are rather like outline sketches, or short stories, about the future. They are intended to catch the attention and the imagination. They are, of course, hypothetical. Scenarios attempt to highlight a particular aspect of the future; they are used to illustrate different choices that we have before us. Is this an alternative future that we want? If so, what do we need to do to bring it about? If not, what do we need to do to avert it? Scenarios help to clarify the choices before us and therefore enhance decision making in the present.

Using different scenarios

The activities in this chapter involve exploration of four different scenarios relating to commonly held views of the future. Each is, of course, an oversimplification. But, as stated above, scenarios are outline sketches with which to catch the attention. The eventual future will, of course, be a mix of different scenarios. It will also vary depending on who we are and where we live on this planet. It is important that pupils study all four scenarios. If time is short, however, it is best to omit the first one.

'*More of the same*' is based on a view of the future which argues that, in fact, not a lot will change. We will be faced with similar sorts of problems nationally and globally, which will be resolved in similar sorts of ways as today. Life will go on much as before: not a lot needs to change.

'*Technological fix*' highlights a view of the future which sees major breakthroughs in science and technology solving many problems. More money is spent on genetic engineering, artificial intelligence, nuclear power, pollution control and space exploration, for example, bringing untold benefits to all.

'*Edge of disaster*' is based on the view that the future will be much worse than today. There may be an increase in famine and poverty worldwide; flooding as a result of global warming; more skin cancers as a result of the holes in the ozone layer. Life will change greatly and never be the same again.

'*Sustainable development*' anticipates major changes in the future in the way people think about the planet and each other. It highlights the need for greater equality and justice than we have now, especially for those most in need, and greater care for the environment as our essential life-upport system.

'*Making choices*', the final activity, gives pupils an opportunity to contrast and compare the different scenarios they have been studying. Which alternative future do they think is the most likely? Which is closest to their own preferred future? How might views of the future differ depending on who you are and where you live on this planet?

Full page photocopiable illustrations of each of the four scenarios are provided with each activity. By exploring each of them in turn, and what people are saying in them, pupils are able to 'visit' different futures. Each activity outline contains both supportive and critical comments about what it's like to live there, as well as a summary paragraph highlighting the main features of each scenario.

NB For the first two scenarios there are urban and rural options. For the last two scenarios there are rich world and poor world options. Initially it is best to only use one of each (that is four in all).

MORE OF THE SAME

Purpose

For pupils to explore, debate and discuss one particular scenario for the future.

Preparation

You will need a copy of Resource 6.1 for each child and copies of either Resource 6.2a or b for groups of children.

Procedure

- Brief the class on the purpose of this activity and go through the instructions and questions on the pupil worksheet with them.
- Pupils work in small groups to discuss the given scenario. They then individually complete their copy of the pupil worksheet.

MORE OF THE SAME: pupils' comments

Sarah: *"It's just not true [that things will stay the same as today] because everything does change, like a plant grows and it changes. We'll find out new things and start reacting to changes."*

Alison: *"Schools are going to change, they'll get more computers. It's stupid to say that things won't change."*

Sameer *"Some things will stay the same but most things will change."*

Sharon: *"We'll have jobs and we're going to learn more things so things will change. Our knowledge will increase"*

Source: Year 5/6 (10 and 11 year olds), Camp Junior School, St. Albans, Hertfordshire

Summary

This future has come about because people feel safe with things as they are and they don't imagine things being very different. It is based on the assumption that things worked reasonably well in the past and will therefore continue to do so in the future. Similar problems will occur and be dealt with in similar ways to today. This future benefits those who are already well off and those who don't like change. It could, on the other hand, lead to one of the edge of disaster scenarios.

Resource 6.1

MORE OF THE SAME: PUPIL WORKSHEET

Look carefully at the first illustration of a possible future in 50 years' time (Resource 6.2a or b). Imagine that you are doing some 'futures fieldwork' and visiting this future with a group of friends to gather information. You can look around to see how things are different and also listen to what people are saying about life in this future.

Source: © Mike McQueen/Impact

1 Do you think people like living in this possible future?

_____

_____

_____

2 What are some of the good things about it?

_____

_____

_____

3 What are some of the difficult things about it?

_____

_____

_____

4 Who will benefit and who will lose in this future?

_____

_____

_____

5 Say why you would or wouldn't like to live in this future.

_____

_____

_____

Source: Brick

Resource 6.2b

Source: Brick

TECHNOLOGICAL FIX

Purpose

For pupils to explore, debate and discuss one particular scenario for the future.

Preparation

You will need a copy of Resource 6.3 for each child and copies of either Resource 6.4a or b for groups of children.

Procedure

- Brief the class on the purpose of this activity and go through the instructions and questions on the pupil worksheet with them.
- Pupils work in small groups to discuss the given scenario. They then individually complete their copy of the pupil worksheet.

TECHNOLOGICAL FIX: pupils' comments

Amir: *"We can find out more about what's happening to the environment."*

Sarah: *"Scientists could change some things but still not stop all the problems."*

Alison: *"We need to care and change our attitudes. Just knowing isn't enough."*

Sarah: *"Technology isn't always helpful. Like before we didn't have so many creams and lipsticks and now we do we test them on animals."*

Ravi: *"We used gas and fumes to kill people in the Gulf War."*

Source: Year 5/6 (10 and 11 year olds), Camp JMI School, St Albans, Hertfordshire

Summary

This future has come about because people felt that rapid growth of science and technology would solve all their problems. It is based on the assumption that what can be invented always should be invented. This future can bring many benefits but can also have many unforeseen consequences. At the same time it also involves dominating nature and thus cuts people off from the natural environment on which all life still depends.

TECHNOLOGICAL FIX: PUPIL WORKSHEET

Look carefully at the second illustration of a possible future in 50 years' time (Resource 6.4a or b). Imagine that you are doing some 'futures fieldwork' and visiting this future with a group of friends to gather information. You can look around to see how things are different and also listen to what people are saying about life in this future.

Source: © E Simanor/Robert Harding

1 Do you think people like living in this possible future?

_____

_____

_____

2 What are some of the good things about it?

_____

_____

3 What are some of the difficult things about it?

_____

_____

_____

4 Who will benefit and who will lose in this future?

_____

_____

_____

5 Say why you would or wouldn't like to live in this future.

_____

_____

_____

Resource 6.4a

Resource 6.4b

Technological fix

Source: Brick

EDGE OF DISASTER

Purpose

For pupils to explore, debate and discuss one particular scenario for the future.

Preparation

You will need a copy of Resource 6.5 for each child and copies of either Resource 6.6a or b for groups of children.

Procedure

● Brief the class on the purpose of this activity and go through the instructions and questions on the pupil worksheet with them.
● Pupils work in small groups to discuss the given scenario. They then individually complete their copy of the pupil worksheet.

EDGE OF DISASTER: pupils' comments

Sameer: *"Because of global warming, the water level is going to rise and cover some islands up. Bangladesh might not survive."*

Amir: *"Trees give us oxygen and we won't have enough."*

Sameer: *"Trees help to suck in the carbon dioxide produced by factories."*

Charlotte: *"Bad things happening in other parts of the world do effect us, it makes us feel sad."*

Lisa: *"It affects you mentally."*

Ruma: *"It would if you lived there."*

Source: Year 5/6 (10 and 11 year olds), Camp JMI School, St Albans, Hertfordshire

---

Summary

This future has come about because governments responsible for making decisions were too slow to act. They worked on the assumption that the problems were not that serious. This assumption was wrong and the scenario shows various disasters, not all of which would necessarily occur at the same time. However, for those living in the 'poor world', many of these disasters are already here as a result of 'rich world' policies. This future doesn't benefit anyone. It can, however, lead governments and people to make major changes in the way they live.

EDGE OF DISASTER: PUPIL WORKSHEET

Look carefully at the third illustration of a possible future in 50 years' time (Resource 6.6a or b). Imagine that you are doing some 'futures fieldwork' and visiting this future with a group of friends to gather information. You can look around to see how things are different and also listen to what people are saying about life in this future.

1 Do you think people like living in this possible future?

_____

_____

_____

2 What are some of the good things about it?

_____

_____

3 What are some of the difficult things about it?

_____

_____

_____

4 Who will benefit and who will lose in this future?

_____

_____

_____

5 Say why you would or wouldn't like to live in this future.

_____

_____

_____

Resource 6.6a

Edge of disaster

SUSTAINABLE DEVELOPMENT

Purpose

For pupils to explore, debate and discuss one particular scenario for the future.

Preparation

You will need a copy of Resource 6.7 for each child and copies of either Resource 6.8a or b for groups of children.

Procedure

- Brief the class on the purpose of this activity and go through the instructions and questions on the pupil worksheet with them.
- Pupils work in small groups to discuss the given scenario. They then individually complete their copy of the pupil worksheet.

SUSTAINABLE DEVELOPMENT: pupils' comments

Moeen:	*"I think some people are more caring, but not enough."*
Sameer:	*"We can use ozone friendly things."*
Ravi:	*"Are these things really ozone friendly?"*
Sameer:	*"It's very hard to care for the environment and to care for people too."*
Sarah:	*"It's greedy people, money is the problem."*
Sameer:	*"If coffee prices rose to say £16 you might say that's a fair price, but when it's cheap it's good for me."*
Ekram:	*"Everybody thinks they're not greedy!"*

Source: Year 5/6 (10 and 11 year olds), Camp JMI School, St Albans, Hertfordshire

Summary

This future has come about because people recognised the need for major change. It is based on the assumption that caring for the environment, other people and future generations also brings a better quality of life in the present. This future brings a less stressful and simpler lifestyle for many people. Developments in science and technology are used by the community to meet their own local needs.

SUSTAINABLE DEVELOPMENT: PUPIL WORKSHEET

Look carefully at the fourth illustration of a possible future in 50 years' time (Resource 6.8a or b). Imagine that you are doing some 'futures fieldwork' and visiting this future with a group of friends to gather information. You can look around to see how things are different and also listen to what people are saying about life in this future.

Source: © Mike Schroder/Still Pictures

1 Do you think people like living in this possible future?

_____

_____

_____

2 What are some of the good things about it?

_____

_____

3 What are some of the difficult things about it?

_____

_____

_____

4 Who will benefit and who will lose in this future?

_____

_____

_____

5 Say why you would or wouldn't like to live in this future.

_____

_____

_____

Resource 6.8a

Resource 6.8b

Sustainable development

Source: Brick

MAKING CHOICES

Purpose

For pupils to reflect on the four scenarios and to compare them with their own preferred futures.

Preparation

The four previous scenarios should all have been studied. Resource 6.9 is needed for the 'Extension' activity.

Procedure

- Pupils work in groups to re-consider each of the four scenarios and then rank them 1 to 4 in the order in which they most *expect* them to come about.
- They then rank them in the order in which they would most *like* them to come about. Is there a difference between the two? Groups report to the whole class on each of their rankings.
- It is important for pupils to realise that people's perceptions of the future will vary depending on factors such as age, gender, race and income. What might older people, disabled people and people on low incomes want to see in the future?
- Pupils conclude by drawing a picture of their own preferred future, complete with comment in speech balloons, like the ones they have just been investigating. How do they also take into account the needs of others?

Extension

- Older or more able pupils can study the quotations in Resource 6.9 from indigenous peoples. [2] How different are their views of the world? What can we learn from this about citizenship?

Indigenous voices

Only when you have felled the last tree, caught the last fish and polluted the last river, will you realise that you can't eat money.

Source: Native American saying

It is an important and special thing to be an Indian. Being an Indian means being able to understand and live with this world in a very special way. It means living with the land, with the animals, with the birds and fish as though they were sisters and brothers. It means saying that the land is an old friend your father knew, your people have always known... To the Indian people our land is really our life.

Source: Richard Nerysoo, Inuit

The white man's advanced technological capacity has occurred as a result of his lack of regard for the spiritual path and for the way of all living things. The white man's desire for material possessions and power has blinded him to the pain he has caused Mother Earth by his quest for what he calls natural resources.

Source: Thomas Banyacya, Hopi village leader

We need to start educating the West... teaching them some social alternatives which place priority on humankind – not profits, not political power, not bombs, but on humanity ... We are on the one hand the most oppressed people on the globe. On the other hand we are the hope for the future of people on the planet.

Source: Thomas Mohawk, writer

We see it like this: it is as if we were all in a canoe travelling through time. If someone begins to make a fire in their part of the canoe, and another begins to pour water inside the canoe, or another begins to piss in the canoe, it will affect us all. And it is the responsibility of each person in the canoe to ensure that it is not destroyed. The destruction of the forest is everyone's concern.

Source: Ailton Krenak,
Brazilian Union of Indian Nations

At first I thought I was fighting to save rubber trees, then I thought I was fighting to save the Amazon rainforest. Now I realise I am fighting for humanity.

Source: Chico Mendes,
rubber tappers' leader

7 | A Sustainable Future

INTRODUCTION

This final activity chapter draws together many of the issues explored earlier in the book. Chapter 4 gave pupils a vocabulary for 'thinking about the future'; Chapter 5 dealt with ways of 'envisioning the future'; and Chapter 6 gave pupils an opportunity to 'choose the future'. This chapter deals with one of the end purposes of futures thinking – the creation of a more 'sustainable society'.

It attempts to illustrate, through four brief case studies, some of the issues that need to be tackled if we want to move away from our present unsustainable lifestyles. Each case study focuses on an aspect of everyday life that needs critical review if we are concerned about the future well-being of this planet.

In 'Projects for a better world' pupils can find out about the sort of organisations concerned with social and political change. What sort of problems do they each attempt to solve and how? Which issues do pupils think are the most important to tackle and why?

'Energy options' introduces some of the issues arising from our daily use of energy. Pupils examine a series of photographs and accompanying text to identify critical questions that need to be asked. They are encouraged to consider options which will have a minimal impact on the environment in the future.

In 'Transport choices' pupils reflect on the costs, both overt and hidden, of using the car as our main form of transportation. In the light of this review they then consider a range of transport alternatives which would be more user-friendly and also ways of redesigning towns to be less reliant on the car.

'Global warming' introduces pupils to the debate about climate change and the possible consequences of this for both people and the environment, now and in the future. In the light of this information the class draws up its own list of 'things we can do'.

PROJECTS FOR A BETTER WORLD

Purpose

For pupils to investigate and discuss the nature of various organisations working to create a better world.

Preparation

Pupils work in pairs and each pair will need a set of the nine cards shown in Resource 7.2. Copies of Resource 7.1 might also be useful for groups of children; alternatively you might prefer to read this out to the class.

Procedure

- Share with the class the explanation about the role of pressure groups in Resource 7.1. What examples of such groups do pupils know of, for example Friends of the Earth, Greenpeace, WWF (environmental issues), Amnesty International, Minority Rights Group (human rights), Oxfam, Christian Aid, Save the Children Fund (development issues)?
- The class then consider nine examples of imaginary organisations working for change. (Actual examples are studied later.)
- This is a ranking activity and the task for each pair is to agree on how they would prioritise the projects, setting the cards out in a diamond shape as shown below. The question to discuss is: Which organisations would you most like to support and why? The first choice goes at the top and the least favoured at the bottom.

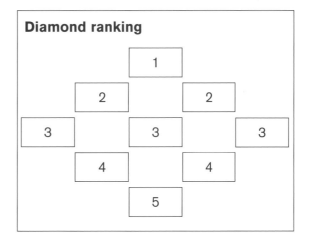

Diamond ranking

- As part of their discussion pairs ask the following questions about each project.
  1 What is the project's focus or concerns?
  2 How does it want the future to be different?
  3 What sort of action is it involved in?
  4 How does it work to create change?
- When each pair has completed their ranking they meet with another pair to share the results. Each takes it in turn to explain their choices.
- Reporting back to the whole class should focus initially on first choices. Which organisations proved most popular and why?

Variation

- Pupils find out what pressure groups, both local and national, exist in their own community. Samples of the organisations' publications will be needed, especially any written for young people. Some organisations can provide speakers who have an educational brief. Only ONE letter should go to any such organisation from a class and be accompanied by a large SAE.
- The class begin by constructing a 'What do we want to know?' list. Some of the questions to ask about a group are:
  1 When was it set up and by whom?
  2 What are its aims?
  3 What sort of issues does it deal with?
  4 How does it do this?
  5 Can young people be involved?
  6 What does its preferable future look like?
  7 How successful has it been in achieving its aims?
- The last two questions are particularly important because a) they relate the work of groups and organisations to images of preferable futures and b) they offer examples of people working successfully together for change.
- Involvement in the activities of particular groups working for change is also an excellent introduction to active citizenship.

Resource 7.1

Pressure groups in society

There are many pressure groups in society today campaigning for change. This may be about local, national or international issues. A pressure group forms when people identify a particular problem or need and then work to publicise this. There are pressure groups on all sorts of issues, from poverty, homelessness and violence, to human rights, war and the environment. They play an important role in drawing people's attention to crucial issues, giving people information they might not otherwise have, working to improve situations, and pressing politicians to pass new laws.

Resource 7.2

Projects for a better world

Living Community is a co-operative project based around a large country house. It was set up by a group of people who believed that by living together they could better support each other. So childcare, all household and garden jobs, and the office work are shared. The community embraces a wide age range, from young children to those who have retired. Living Community's vision of the future is one in which people learn to live, work and play more harmoniously together. They know this is often hard but believe that we can only change the world by changing ourselves.

Source: © Neil Morrison/WWF-UK

Resource 7.2 *continued*

Working Together is a network which identifies the needs of the local community and then helps set up new business ventures to meet those needs. The emphasis is on local ownership and local expertise. So far the network has helped groups to set up a community restaurant, a wholefood shop, a bookshop and a small market where locally grown fruit and vegetables can be sold. People are thus coming to realise that the community can be more self-sufficient and responsible for meeting its own needs. Working Together's vision of the future is one in which people work co-operatively together to meet as many of their own needs as possible.

Source: © Photo from www.JohnBirdsall.co.uk

Source: © Julio Etchart/Panos Pictures

Justice Now is an international organisation which reports on abuses of human rights in the world. It draws attention to cases of injustice against both individuals and groups – whether at the hands of governments, the military or other powerful bodies. It publicises the cases of those who have been abused, wrongfully imprisoned, tortured or silenced, and argues for their release. Justice Now's vision of the future is one in which all people are free and equal in the eyes of the law. It believes that putting pressure on unjust governments can bring about changes.

Green World is an environmental action group which has branches throughout the country. It is concerned about the problems of acid rain, global warming, the ozone layer, industrial pollution and the dumping of toxic waste. Its vision of the future is one in which people naturally choose to take more care of the environment. It aims to publicise 'crimes against the environment' by carrying out dramatic publicity stunts which will catch newspaper headlines and TV coverage. Green World believes that environmental concern will grow as public opinion changes.

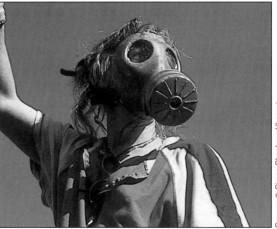

Source: © Simon Shepheard/Impact

Resource 7.2   *Continued*

Fair Shares is a group which campaigns against world poverty especially in Africa, Asia and Latin America. It is concerned about underdevelopment and the way in which the rich countries of the world help to cause this. Its slogan is 'Enough for need but not for greed'. It helps local groups in Third World countries set up the projects they think will be the most useful, from health care and water supply to new housing projects. Fair Share's vision of the future is one in which no one group of countries is rich at the expense of others. It believes rich countries need to follow a simpler lifestyle.

Source: © Tricia Spanner

Source: © Jeremy Nichou/Impact

Stop Racism! is a national organisation which exists to fight racial prejudice and discrimination. It calls for full equal opportunities in education and at work so that members of ethnic minority groups are fully represented at all levels of the community. It publicises cases of racial harassment and assault, and the extent of racism in society. It works with both black and white people to change people's attitudes and behaviour, and to create a fairer and more equal society for all. Stop Racism's vision of the future is one in which racial justice and racial equality are taken as normal.

Women Space is an organisation which exists to combat discrimination against women, at work and in the community. It publicises examples of successful women's projects and offers advice and legal support. It also draws attention to ways in which everyone can benefit from greater sexual equality. Women Space's vision of the future is one in which women have complete equality with men in all aspects of life and in which gender is no longer used as an excuse for discrimination. It believes that change comes about by women working to identify their own needs.

Source: © Photo from www.JohnBirdsall.co.uk

Resource 7.2 *Continued*

Resolving Conflict is a local organisation which helps people to learn about more peaceful conflict resolution. It has helped neighbours settle disputes, and run courses on how to deal with conflicts at home and at work. It is also involved in mediating over cases of racial and sexual harassment, and helping to solve conflicts, for example, between property developers and local people, and in schools. Resolving Conflict's vision of the future is one in which people have learnt skills of successful conflict resolution and can apply them in daily life. They believe such change is possible through the training of mediators, as well as training people to resolve conflicts for themselves.

Source: © Photo from www.JohnBirdsall.co.uk

Source: © Peter Arkell/Impact

Growing Older is a national organisation set up to highlight the needs of older and elderly people and to stress the important contribution they can make to the community. Far from feeling that life is over when retirement age is reached, the emphasis is on valuing the expertise and wisdom of older people. Growing Older's vision of the future is one in which older people are well cared for by the community and in which their contribution is fully recognised. It believes that change will occur through encouraging more opportunities for young and older people to do things together.

ENERGY OPTIONS

Purpose

To explore some of the issues raised by our uses of energy and to consider energy options for the future.

Preparation

Previous work on future scenarios (see Chapter 6) will set these issues in a broader context. Each group of pupils will need copies of the photograph on Resource 7.3 (minus text) and the photos on Resource 7.4, each mounted on a large sheet of paper, plus the text in Resource 7.5.

Procedure

- Pupils work in small groups. Each group has one of the photographs shown in Resources 7.3 and 7.4. They study and discuss their photograph carefully. What questions arise? The group write their questions around the border of the photograph. An example of this is shown in Resource 7.3. Each of the five are mounted on the wall with their questions around them.
- Next each group has a full set of photos and a copy of Resource 7.5 in front of them. The task is to match the photos to the text. Which goes with which? Can the group arrange their photos in such a way that they 'tell a story' about energy choices?
- Which of their questions are answered by the accompanying text? Which questions still require further research?
- Each group prepares a statement about their preferred energy options for the future. Is there anything they can do to help bring about their preferred energy future?

Sellafield told: clean up or close down

Paul Brown, *Environment Correspondent*

Government safety watchdogs yesterday threatened to shut down commercial activities at Britain's biggest nuclear site, at Sellafield, after damning reports set out a catalogue of "systematic management failures" which allowed workers to routinely falsify quality assurance records.

Three highly critical reports from the Nuclear Installations Inspectorate (NII) demanded that senior management of British Nuclear Fuels (BNFL) be held responsible for the comprehensive failure of safety culture at the site, in Cumbria.

Laurence Williams, NII chief inspector, said: "It's no use sacking a few production workers. Responsibility must start at the top."

But the government decided to take no immediate action, instead giving Hugh Collum, the new BNFL chairman, two months to come up with sweeping management changes to restore confidence in the company.

A Downing Street spokesman said: "This is serious, it is unacceptable and something needs to be done about it. Something will be done about it."

Number 10 issued a statement supporting the actions of energy minister Helen Liddell. "I have asked Mr Collum for comprehensive and radical suggestions for change, which will deliver the management that the company needs, within two months," she said. "The review should regard no one at no level in the organisation as out of bounds. I know that Hugh Collum shares my view of the need for change."

The reports follow a series of safety incidents at Sellafield which prompted the inspection. At the same time, a set of falsified data was found involving mixed plutonium and uranium fuel (Mox) which was being manufactured at Sellafield for use in Japanese reactors.

The Japanese discovered they had been misled just before the fuel was loaded into their reactors in December and said they could no longer "trust" the company. They are demanding that Britain sends armed ships to Japan to bring the suspect fuel home.

The section of the plant where the falsification occurred is shut down and will not be allowed to restart until the NII is satisfied that the recommendations have been implemented.

This has placed in jeopardy government plans to sell off 49% of BNFL, which hhave been postponed until after the election. It has also made it near impossible for BNFL to justify opening its £300m Mox plant which needs ministerial approval. The company must prove it has orders for the fuel, but its main customer is Japan.

Poor design of the plant, the tedium of the job, and the ease with which the computer dating logging system was manipulated were all blamed for the falsification problem.

Five production workers had been sacked; but despite the NII's conclusions that management was to blame, no other action has been taken. The report says the site is safe but "the standard of achievement was only just tolerable".

Individual workers were blamed for safety incidents when "there was a trail of poor standards tolerated by management". The attitude of blaming workers for management failures had hit morale, the report said.

Mr Williams said unless the company comes up with solutions within two months he will order the closure of "commercial operations from which the company makes its money."

BNFL chief executive John Taylor and Chris Loughlin, the BNFL board director responsible for Mox business, both of whom could lose their jobs, were yesterday in Japan trying to convince customers that Mox was safe and they should buy some after all.

Mr Taylor said: "We deeply regret these events and the problems they have caused for our customers. We now need to get on with implementing the action plan and restoring our credibility."

Brian Watson, head of the Sellafield site, said: "This has been a shock for us all. It is not good news for our Mox business. We have to drive forward and change the [safety] culture. We have to remember that nobody is saying that Sellafield is unsafe. Safety is, and will always be, our number one priority."

Pete Roche, a Greenpeace nuclear campaigner, said "These reports are a shocking exposé of Sellafield's plutonium business. This is a company dealing with one of the most hazardous materials known to mankind and they have been shown to be guilty of lax management and falsifying records.

"The government must act decisively to end nuclear reprocessing and also refuse BNFL the go-ahead to start commercial production of Mox fuel."

• British Nuclear Fuels and BNFL Engineering are to face prosecution over breaches of safety regulations at Sellafield, the health and safety executive announced last night. The allegations follow an incident on March 11 last year when nitric acid was released at the plant, injuring two workers.

Source: *The Guardian*, 19 February 2000

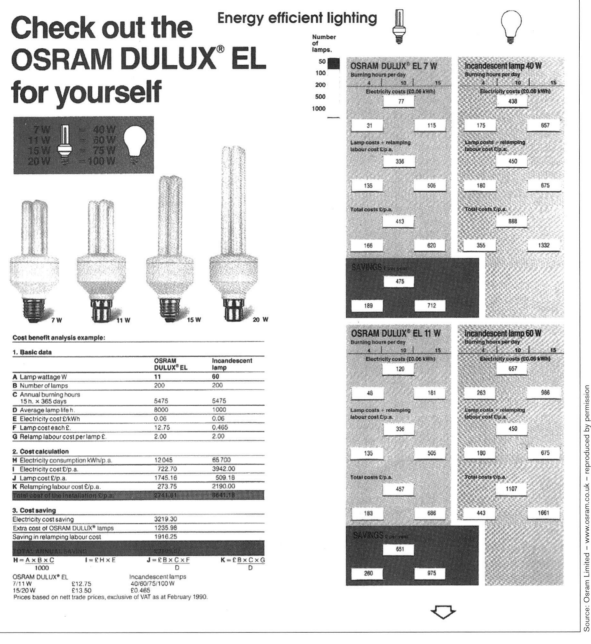

Source: Osram Limited – www.osram.co.uk – reproduced by permission

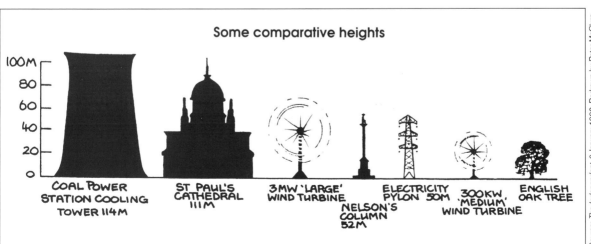

Some comparative heights

Source: The Independent, 6 January 1992. Redrawn by Peter McClure

Resource 7.3

Asking questions

Are they noisy?

Where was this photograph taken?

How much electricity do they produce?

How tall are these turbines?

Source: © David Lawson/WWF-UK

Is it in Britain?

Who owns the windfarm?

Whose idea was it?

Who uses it?

Who built them?

Do the local people like them?

How do they work?

What happens if the wind doesn't blow?

Why is it called a windfarm?

Resource 7.4

Source: © Edward Parker/WWF-UK

Source: © Barry Lewis/Network

Source: © EPL/Martin Bond

Source: © Mike Schroder/Still Pictures

Resource 7.5

ENERGY ISSUES

Uses of energy

Whenever we turn on a switch, eat a meal or buy something from the shop we are depending on manufactured energy. We use it all the time: to keep warm, to cook, to watch TV, to travel, to grow food, to manufacture things. Make a list of all the ways in which you use such energy during the course of a day.

Sources of energy

Often we use energy in the form of electricity: for heat, light, to run the TV or computer. To create electricity a source of fuel is needed. These are either i) fossil fuels such as coal, oil, gas and uranium; or ii) renewable sources, such as the sun, wind, water and geothermal. Fossils fuels are finite, that is they will run out one day. Renewable sources, as the name suggests, go on and on.

Energy problems

The ways in which we produce and use energy cause a variety of problems. Fumes from cars in cities create smog and cause eye and lung complaints; acid rain caused by pollution from coal and oil fired power stations, poisons rivers, lakes, soil and trees; radioactive waste from nuclear power stations has to be stored safely and accidents, such as that at Chernobyl, affect areas thousands of kilometres away; increased CO_2 in the atmosphere from the burning of fossil fuels is contributing to global warming.

Energy options

The way in which we create and use energy now will affect the lives of those in the future. Energy choices are largely the result of government decisions. Predictions are made about energy needs and how to meet these. Currently the government's emphasis is on fossil fuels. However, people can make choices about how much energy they use and in what form they want it.

FOSSIL FUELS

Coal

Until the 1950s coal was the chief fuel for power stations, ships, trains and heating. There are various by-products of coal such as chemicals, plastics, fertilisers and paints. Globally there are more coal reserves than any other fossil fuel. Burning coal in a power station creates gases such as CO_2 which contribute to global warming. New small power stations are the most efficient, especially when the 'waste' steam or water is used to provide local heating.

Oil

Oil has been the most widely used fossil fuel since it replaced coal in the 1950s. Petrol, aircraft fuel, nylon and plastics, all come from oil. Most oil reserves are in the Middle East. When oil spills occur from supertankers, such as the *Exxon Valdez* off Alaska, the damage to the coastline and wildlife can be enormous. World oil consumption has risen from 11 million barrels a day in 1950 to 65 million barrels a day now.

Uranium

Uranium is the fuel used in nuclear power stations. All mining can damage the environment, but waste from uranium mining is also poisonous. Whilst nuclear power stations emit no hazardous gases, electricity generated from nuclear power is more expensive than other forms. There is the even greater problem of storing radioactive nuclear waste for thousands of years.

NUCLEAR POWER

Origins

Uranium atoms are split in the reactor of a nuclear power station to release enormous amounts of energy. Uranium produces far more energy than the same amount of oil or coal. It was originally argued that nuclear power would provide electricity much more cheaply than oil or coal fired power stations.

Advantages

For a long time nuclear power was thought to be the answer to all our future energy problems. Its advantage over coal and oil fired stations is that it produces no CO_2 and so does not contribute to acid rain or global warming. Some people argue that nuclear power is the only real energy option for the future because renewable sources of energy (wind, wave, solar) will never produce enough power to meet our needs.

Disadvantages

There are, however, various dangers associated with nuclear power. The accident at Chernobyl spread radiation thousands of kilometres across the world. Neither has any safe long-term solution been found to the storage of nuclear waste which needs to be stored safely for at least 250,000 years. Some countries dump it in the sea, some store it underground. It is also one of the most expensive ways of generating electricity. There are very few nuclear power stations now being built in the world.

ENERGY EFFICIENCY

More for less

One of the easiest ways to solve energy problems is to use less energy in the first place. This can be done by making homes, electrical appliances and industry more energy efficient. If the energy we use does more work for us than before it is less wasteful: we save energy, which means we need less of it, and pay less for it. One report suggests we could cut our fuel bills in this way by between 20% and 60%. If demand drops, so does the need for new power stations.

At home

Most houses are very energy inefficient. Heat leaks out through windows, roofs and walls. Good roof and wall insulation means houses hold heat longer. 'Superinsulated' houses in Sweden and the USA use 50% less fuel to keep warm as ordinary houses, even in severe winters. For this to become the norm, stricter building regulations need to be introduced and improvements made to domestic appliances to achieve greater energy efficiency. Compact fluorescent lightbulbs cost more but last up to 15 times as long as an ordinary lightbulb and use 80% less electricity.

At work

Vast amounts of fuel and electricity are wasted in heating and lighting offices, stores and warehouses. Often light and heating are centrally controlled and left on when not needed. Redesigning buildings to be energy efficient could result in savings of 40% on fuel bills. In many industries, from making paper to making steel, energy savings can be made. What is now needed is a change of heart in industry, business, government and in the home, so that energy efficiency is seen as normal.

Resource 7.5 *continued*

RENEWABLE ENERGY

Wind power

For centuries windmills have been used to turn machinery, whether to grind flour or to pump water. Wind turbines provide a quick and cheap way to generate electricity. Britain is well suited to wind power, especially in the windy and hilly west. Turbines are sited together in what is called a wind park. It has been calculated that wind power could provide 20% or more of Britain's energy needs. Some people feel that such wind parks would be unattractive and that they would spoil the view.

Water power

Energy can also be provided by the sea with special rafts off the coast. These collect the power of the waves and operate turbines which are connected to the shore by cables. Tidal barrages can also be used to generate electricity as the tide goes in and out. The Severn estuary could provide a site for such a barrage. In mountainous areas hydro-electric power can be generated. Here water is stored in reservoirs and falls through huge pipes to turn a turbine in the power station.

Solar power

The sun is also a valuable source of energy. Solar collectors sited on south facing walls and roofs depend on brightness rather than direct sunlight. They can absorb sufficient heat to meet about 50% of domestic hot water and heating needs. Solar heating can thus be used to supplement other existing domestic heating. Creating electricity from solar energy is more difficult but solar cells can be used to power some appliances.

TRANSPORT CHOICES

Purpose

To explore different ways of resolving traffic problems for the future.

Preparation

Copies of the photographs in Resource 7.6 and the facts in Resources 7.7, 7.8 and 7.9 are needed for each group. Pupils will also need photographs of cars taken from newspapers and magazines.

Procedure

- Pupils work in small groups to look at the photographs in Resource 7.6, the facts about cars in Resource 7.7 and the pictures of cars from magazines.
- Groups prepare and present to the class their own statement about the disadvantages of the car.
- Next they consider the photographs in Resource 7.6 and the information about alternatives in Resource 7.8, and prepare a group statement about the advantages of these.
- Then the group looks at the information in Resource 7.9 on how transport systems might be improved in the future. Using what they have already learnt, and the photos as accompanying illustrations, they design an imaginary town that embodies the best of transport choices. Alternatively they could redesign the transport system of their local town. This can be drawn as a land-use map or as a series of illustrations. Which forms of transport cause least pollution? Which carry most people? Which take up least space? How could houses, workplaces and shops be resited to reduce journeys to a minimum?
  NB Pupils with internet access might like to visit the Rocky Mountain Institute web site at www.rmi.org which contains information on environment and people 'friendly' design and alternatives to the car.

Resource 7.6

Source: © Pierre Gleizes/Still Pictures

Source: © Mark Edwards/Still Pictures

Source: © Mark Edwards/Still Pictures

Source: © Mark Edwards/Still Pictures

Resource 7.7

Cars: the hidden costs

Our quality of life depends on transport. Most of us travel every day, even if only locally. And we need an efficient transport system to support a strong and prosperous economy. But in turn, the way we travel is damaging our towns and cities and harming our countryside. As demand for transport grows, we are even changing the very climate of our planet.

Cars in particular have revolutionised the way we live, bringing great flexibility and widening horizons... But the way we are using our cars has a price – for our health, for the economy and for the environment.

Congestion and unreliability of journeys add to the costs of business... The CBI has put the cost to the British economy at around £15 billion every year...

In the UK, emissions of CO_2 from road transport are the fastest growing contributor to climate change – the greatest global environmental threat facing the international community.

Three in 10 homes in Britain don't have a car – some 13 million people. The advantages of owning a car aren't available to them. Increased traffic and speed have made our streets more threatening for pedestrians and cyclists. Children's freedom to play, or to walk or cycle to school unaccompanied has been severely curtailed. Twenty years ago, nearly one in three five to 10 years olds made their own way to school. Now only one child in nine does.

The way we travel is making us a less healthy nation. Coronary heart disease is the biggest killer of adults in this country. Part of the blame is that we drive too much when we could walk or cycle.

Road traffic is a major contributor to air pollution. Up to 24,000 vulnerable people are estimated to die prematurely each year, and similar numbers are admitted to hospital, because of exposure to air pollution, much of which is due to road traffic.

Although serious road casualties have declined, too many people are still killed or seriously injured on our roads (more than 120 people every day in 1997)...

Source: Extracts from 'A New Deal for Transport: Better for Everyone', Government White Paper on the Future of Transport, 1998

Resource 7.8

Transport alternatives

In a public opinion survey about traffic in London, 80% of people were concerned about the effects of exhaust fumes, air pollution and accidents. 50% felt drivers would switch to public transport if this was improved and more road space was given to pedestrians, buses and cycles.

Public transport uses less fuel, creates less pollution and uses up less space on the road than cars. An underground metro can carry 70,000 people per hour past a given point; surface rail can carry 50,000 people; a bus or tram on a separate lane can carry 30,000 people; a lane of cars (even if full) can move only 8,000 people per hour.

In order to reduce traffic, several cities have turned to light rail or metro systems, such as the Docklands Light railway in London. In Cambridge and Oxford there have also been experiments with 'trishaws' – licensed rickshaws used instead of taxis.

Cycling and walking are the most economical, clean and space saving forms of transport. The only fuel required is your last meal. Making cycling practical requires the provision of continuous safe routes through cities which are kept quite separate from cars. In the Netherlands, 30% of journeys to work and 60% of journeys to school are made by bicycle. An extensive network of cycle ways

Resource 7.8   *continued*

make this possible. In Denmark, Japan and Germany there are bike-and-ride facilities that enable people to take their bikes on public transport.

Well managed public transport can help both people and the environment. Curitiba in south-eastern Brazil has earned international praise for its public transport programme. It has few traffic jams despite having more cars per person than most other Brazilian cities – 70% of its commuters travel by bus. A system of express, inter-district and 'feeder' buses provide a regular, closely linked service. Terminals at 2km intervals are equipped with newspaper stands, public telephones, post offices and shops. There is a single fare for all journeys within the city limits, and interchangeable tickets on all routes.

Resource 7.9

Redesign your town

As much as a fifth of the land in a modern city is devoted to cars. All governments since 1945 have spent more on the private motorist than on pedestrians, cyclists and users of public transport. The road building and motor industries also put pressure on the government to build more roads.

In order to promote alternative transport schemes encouragement is needed from central government, local councils, pressure groups and individuals. Many exciting examples of schemes which attempt to resolve the congestion caused by cars can be found.

The way in which cities are laid out has often come to reflect the needs of the motorist. Shops, parking and workplaces are all designed for motorists rather than pedestrians, cyclists or bus users. It is taken for granted that using a car is normal and that everyone expects to have to travel some distance to get to work or shops.

What is needed is a major rethink about the layout of cities. Cities that spread over a large area encourage the use of cars. Cities that are more compact are less likely to require cars. If homes, work and shops are close together, people do not need to use cars. If, on the other hand, people live a long way from work or from the shops, they are more likely to use a car.

What might the future look like if cities were not dominated by cars? Imagine a series of concentric zones. The centre would be for use by pedestrians and passengers arriving by metro or tram. Moving outwards from the centre, streets would then be shared by pedestrians, cyclists, trams and buses. Further out cars would be allowed, but well-placed bus and rail stops would offer a quicker way of getting round. Finally express bus and train routes would link outlying suburbs with each other and to the main city area. Car parking would be increasingly available as you moved away from the city centre.

GLOBAL WARMING

Purpose

To highlight some of the key issues related to global warming and to consider how present action can affect future trends.

Preparation

Previous work on global warming would be useful. This could be linked to 'Energy options' (pages 79–84) and 'Transport choices' (pages 84–89). Pupils will need copies of Resources 7.10 to 7.15.

Procedure

- Pupils study copies of Resources 7.10 to 7.14, which contain information about the causes and consequences of global warming. They then work on the following tasks.

- They research and prepare the front page of a newspaper for 2020 under the headline 'The crisis hots up'. This has a local, national and international section. It includes illustrations and news reports about the effects of global warming. These should then be used to make a wall display.

- Global warming will be in the news for a long time to come. The class keeps its own folder about this issue and the action that people can take to help avert it. The folder can include newspaper clippings, articles and illustrations, as well as records of individual and class action taken.

- The class draws up their own list of 'Things we can do' and then compares this with the suggestions in Resource 7.15. They prepare a mini-presentation to give to other classes, to use in assembly or with parents and governors.

Resource 7.10

THE HEAT IS ON

Daffodils that bloom before Christmas, lawns that grow all year round, and the demise of white winters: it's not hard to spot the impact of global warming. Of course, a few balmy winters do not necessarily make a greenhouse of our planet. Britain's weather has always been a bit odd, after all. Nevertheless, these observations – combined with scientific reports of melting Alpine permafrost and glaciers, rising sea levels and soaring summer temperatures – paint a bleak picture. Earth is overheating, alarmingly.

Arid lands are spreading; agricultural production faces a slump; diseases such as malaria are destined to increase while millions of people are likely to be displaced by rising sea levels. And that's looking on the bright side, for these are the minimum likely impacts of current rates of warming. In fact... it is now becoming clear that change will not be gradual or steady. It will be a deadly, exponential acceleration.

Nor is this the talk of scaremongering greenies. These predictions come from cautious, sober scientists. Yet they are still ignored by our leaders who continue to talk of trading in debts of 'emission gases' so their voters can avoid altering lifestyles that threaten to devastate our planet. It is perhaps the starkest modern example we have of politicians' inability to act responsibly and effectively. They are fiddling, as our world burns ever more intensely

Source: *The Observer*, 30 January 2000

Understanding the greenhouse effect

The Earth's atmosphere is made up of various gases all of which are vital to life. The atmosphere also plays an important role in keeping the temperature of the Earth just right for life. It is like the glass of a greenhouse. The sun's warmth passes easily through and the glass then traps the warmth inside. This is the 'greenhouse effect': it is necessary for life to exist, but things are now changing.

It is now thought that human actions may be altering the balance of the gases in the atmosphere, particularly as a result of industrial activity. Various gases which trap heat are being released into the Earth's atmosphere so that it has been steadily warming up. Carbon dioxide (CO_2) is the most important of these 'greenhouse gases'. It comes from burning coal and oil in power stations, car exhausts, and burning wood for fuel or to clear forest. Other gases are nitrous oxide (N_2O) which comes from burning fossil fuels and through the use of fertilisers which contain nitrogen. Chlorofluorocarbons (or CFCs for short) are man-made gases, which come from some spray cans, refrigerators, air-conditioners and some foam plastics.

When all the greenhouse gases are added together we find that Europe and North America (25% of the world's population) produce 65% of the gases. Africa, Asia and Latin America (75% of the world's population) produce only 35% of these gases. This raises the question of who is most responsible for global warming? A succession of unusually warm years in the 1990s indicates that global warming is already here.

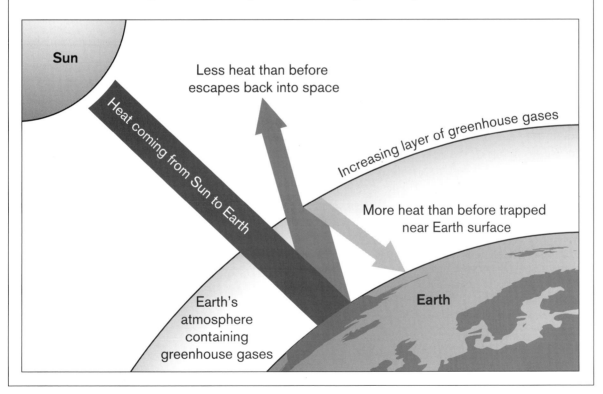

Sun

Less heat than before escapes back into space

Heat coming from Sun to Earth

Increasing layer of greenhouse gases

More heat than before trapped near Earth surface

Earth's atmosphere containing greenhouse gases

Earth

Resource 7.12

Consequences of global warming

Scientists generally agree that average world temperatures will rise by between 1–3°C by 2030. This may not sound much, but the world as a whole could become warmer than at any time in history. The effects of this will vary from country to country and place to place.

Global warming will mean warmer oceans and thus a rise in sea levels. Satellites have already detected a shrinkage of the Arctic ice cap over the last 10 years. As oceans rise, low-lying coastland will be subjected to flooding, wave damage and the salt will ruin cropland and water supplies. Look at the map of Britain opposite to see which areas are most threatened. Densely settled river deltas, as in Egypt and Bangladesh, are also particularly under threat as are low-lying islands such as the Maldives. Coastal fisheries, sea defences, ports, beaches and tourist resorts will be affected.

As the Earth's atmosphere warms up, weather patterns will be affected leading to more extremes and 'freak' weather conditions. Some places will have higher temperatures which may bring drought to existing farmlands. Other areas may have more storms and rainfall so that crops will increasingly be put at risk. The world's bread basket, the American Mid-West, is likely to become much drier leading to drops in grain yield. Natural vegetation and animals will also be affected as their habitats are changed by global warming.

Rich countries will be much better able to deal with these changes, whether in building flood defences or offering help to farmers and householders. It is in poorer countries that the effects of global warming will be most seriously felt. Governments there will only be able to offer limited help.

Source: 'Planet in Peril', *The Observer*, 8 April 1990. Redrawn by Peter McClure

Resource 7.13

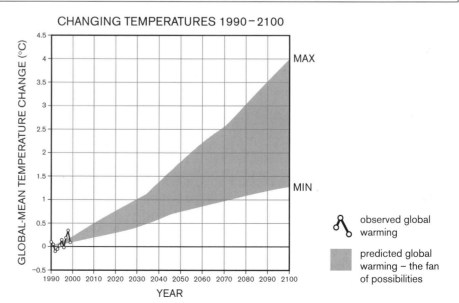

CHANGING TEMPERATURES 1990–2100

Source: Based on *The Science of Climate Change*, TML Wigley, Pew Center for Global Climate Change, 1999. Adapted by TML Wigley

Resource 7.14

Source: © Denis Thorpe. Reproduced with permission of *The Guardian*, 26 February 1991

Source: © Daniel Dancer/Still Pictures

Source: © Kittprempool-UNEP/Still Pictures

Resource 7.15

Things we can do

Saving energy at home

Since many greenhouse gases come from the burning of fossil fuels, any reduction in energy demand is important.

- Turn off lights and heating when they are not needed.
- Use electrical appliances less.
- Buy appliances with a high energy efficiency rating.
- Put on a sweater instead of turning up the heat.
- Insulate roofs, doors, walls and windows well.

Saving energy on the road

Since car and vehicle exhausts contribute to global warming, using the car less is helpful.

- Walk or cycle rather than using the car.
- Use public transport whenever possible.
- Shop locally for local products.
- Keep the car in good condition.
- Drive the car as smoothly as possible.

Saving energy by recycling

Many materials can be recycled and using things again limits the energy (and raw materials) needed to make new items.

- Save old paper and newspapers to recycle.
- Save bottles and aluminium cans to recycle.
- Avoid items which have excess packaging.
- Re-use envelopes and use recycled paper.

Keep planting things

Trees and green plants take in CO_2 and play an important part in reducing the amount of this gas in the atmosphere.

- Plant trees in the garden.
- Plant trees in the school grounds.
- Grow lots of indoor plants.
- Protect native trees.

Public opinion

Putting pressure on manufacturers, shop owners and governments can have an important effect in slowing global warming.

- Take action as a class or whole school.
- Press for local tree planting projects.
- Meet council representatives.
- Write to and meet local MPs.

Taking Things Further

INTRODUCTION

This chapter contains four short annotated bibliographies giving further information on useful classroom resources, teacher references, addresses and journals. The emphasis is mainly on books available in the UK. The Appendix which follows contains Oxfam's curriculum for global citizenship.

Two dilemmas arise in identifying resources. The first is that there is an imbalance between citizenship materials for pupils and for teachers. There are still more of the latter than the former. More widely, of course, there are a variety of materials that can be used for citizenship education although not expressly written for that purpose. Secondly, while educational resources on social and global issues are quite plentiful, those which also explicitly take a futures perspective are not. Many materials may therefore help pupils explore the current state of society and the planet, but leave unanswered questions about probable or preferable alternative futures.

This dissonance between implicit and explicit consideration of the future is an important one which has been explored further by Noel Gough.[1] His investigation into educational documents revealed three sorts of common references to the future – 'tacit, token or taken-for-granted', as shown below.

Futures in education

- **Tacit futures** – all those which are implied but never clearly stated in a document, for example references to 'preparation for adult life' or 'the future of society'. Such futures are not defined or clarified in any way and are thus virtually invisible except to the practised eye.
- **Token futures** – all those which involve some passing rhetorical reference, but which lack substance or explanation, for example the need to 'educate for the future'. Such futures often involve uncritical clichés. This might be about 'citizenship for tomorrow', but what sort of future that might be is never explored.
- **Taken-for-granted futures** – all those which do describe a particular future but assume that it is the only one, with no suggestion that others are possible. The most common example of this is the belief that the future will be a glossier hi-tech version of today.

The few available topic books that touch on the future tend to be about particular issues, for example, the environment, energy, endangered species, transport, with just a final page or short section on the future. This is generally a token or taken-for-granted view of the future too. A reviewer of one such series of books noted that:

"The books are fairly described as 'optimistic and thought provoking'. This hints at one potential problem... Brief accounts of new and future 'technological fixes' in food production, the transmitting and storage of data, the generation of power, the treatment of disease, risk portraying a world floating free of economics and politics: problems simply line up to be cracked by teams of eager scientists."[2]

Whilst the present situation, and the past causes, of current situations (local and global) need careful explanation, the future warrants more than a token reference at the end: it now needs to be a part of the main text. What appears to be the probable future in relation to this issue? What are the choices and alternatives open to people? What are some of their preferable futures? What sort of action for change are people involved in? What choices do we need to make in relation to this particular issue?

CLASSROOM RESOURCES

Brown, M ed (1996)
Our World, Our Rights: Teaching About Rights and Responsibilities in the Primary School, *Amnesty International*

This book is an excellent compendium of ideas and practical classroom activities aimed at introducing children to issues of human rights and responsibilities. It can be used with 8-14 year olds and is a valuable resource book for citizenship education. It looks at: what rights look like in daily life; rights in different parts of the world and at other times in history; the responsibilities which accompany rights; the action needed to defend one's own rights and those of others. The activities encourage the skills of discussion, empathy, co-operation, negotiation and consensus.

Dorion, C & Kendell, P (1999)
Lessons in Life: Sustainable Development Resources for Primary Teachers, *WWF-UK;*
Brook, P (1999)
Lessons in Life: Sustainable Development Resources for Secondary Teachers, *WWF-UK*

These two booklets are aimed at primary and secondary teachers respectively and each follows the same format. They begin with a clear definition of education for sustainable development and an explanation of its importance to schools, together with a list of key concepts central to sustainable development. Each curriculum subject is then taken in turn to show the connections it has with issues of sustainability. Useful illustrations of classroom work are given for each subject. A good first introduction to this aspect of citizenship.

Burns, S & Lamont, G (1995)
Values and Visions: Spiritual Development and Global Awareness in the Primary School, *Hodder*

This is an exciting and illuminating resource book for teachers which shows how personal, social and global issues are interrelated, and how they can be explored in experiential and participatory ways in the classroom. It contains a feast of ideas and should be on the shelf of every staffroom. Whilst aimed at primary schools it is an equally valuable resource for PSHE, citizenship and RE with lower secondary pupils. Four key areas of experience are explored: a sense of self; a sense of community; valuing the Earth, and developing openness to suffering and joy.

Clough, N & Holden, C (2001)
Education for Citizenship: A Practical Handbook for Teachers of Children Aged 7-14, *Routledge*

This book provides practical advice for teachers on how to implement citizenship education and the teaching of democracy. It is illustrated with examples of recent classroom work and has photocopiable materials to support all curriculum areas. Key themes are: social and moral education;

handling topical issues; understanding and involvement in the community; development of skills and knowledge required for democratic participation; understanding racism and challenging stereotypes. Links between theory and practice encourage a reflective and creative approach to learning and teaching.

Fountain, S (1990)
Education for Development: A Teacher's Resource for Global Learning, *Hodder*

This is another excellent resource book for both primary and secondary teachers which aims to promote the development of co-operative skills and a global perspective in the classroom. It provides a conceptual framework for global citizenship and contains a large number of practical classroom activities. These are divided into five sections which in turn explore: interdependence; images and perceptions; social justice; conflict and conflict resolution; change and the future.

Fountain, S (1990)
Learning Together: Global Education 4-7, *WWF-UK*

The value of this book lies in the way it shows how notions of global citizenship can be applied to work with younger pupils. In particular it focuses on the attitudes, values and skills which are needed for getting on creatively with others and shows how these need to underpin any notion of social relating and community. It also focuses on ways of developing the essential skills of self-esteem, communication and co-operation.

Pike, G & Selby, D (1995)
Reconnecting: From National to Global Curriculum, *WWF-UK*

Might a national curriculum also be a nationalistic one? Indeed, might citizenship be used to promote nationalistic aims? This rich and practical resource book is an antidote to any such possibility. It contains: a four-dimensional model of global education; classroom activities for the 11-16 age range in eight curriculum areas; examples of curriculum reform in the UK, Canada and Australia; and whole school case studies on the implementation of global citizenship. Every secondary school should have a copy.

Steiner, M (1993)
***Learning from Experience: Co-operative
Learning and Global Education**,*
Trentham Books

This resource book, as the title suggests,
provides a range of classroom activities – all
of which explore the global element of
citizenship. These activities are designed to
promote affirmation, communication,
empathy and critical thinking. There are also
useful sections on approaches to
assessment, organising learning, groupwork
and topic work, as well as detailed examples
of how such active learning with a global
focus is applicable to most subject areas of
the curriculum.

Symons, G (1998)
***Making it Happen: Agenda 21 and Schools**,*
WWF-UK

Local Agenda 21 is concerned with
promoting more sustainable practice in the
local community in all areas of life. It lies at
the heart of active and responsible citizenship
and is a process that all schools can engage

with. This book provides case studies and
ideas for activities to explore local issues of
environment and development. It encourages
pupils to ask questions about how decisions
are made, how they themselves can influence
change, and what consequences different
choices will have on themselves and others.
Citizenship and education for sustainable
development are woven together in this
practical book.

TEACHER REFERENCES

Brown, L *et al* (1999)
***Vital Signs 1999-2000: The Environmental
Trends that are Shaping our Future**, Earthscan*

This annual publication from the Worldwatch
Institute in Washington is one of the best on-
going summaries of contemporary global
trends. Each is set out in a double-page
layout with easy to read accompanying
graphs and statistics. Trends reported on in
this edition include: food; agricultural
resources; energy; climatic change;
economics; transport; communications;
social and military matters. There is also a
special features section with more detailed
information on pesticide resistant crops,
government corruption and malnutrition.

Button, J (1995)
***The Radicalism Handbook: A Complete
Guide to the Radical Movement in the 20th
Century**, Cassell*

Contains over 360 biographies of 20th
century radicals, including freethinkers,
suffragists, pacifists, Third World
liberationists, campaigners for civil and
human rights, and global and environmental
activists. The entries have been selected to
give a balance of men and women, as well
as thinkers and activists from the rich world
and the poor world. The book also profiles
over 80 radical groups and movements that
helped shape the 20th century. Highlights
the crucial role of radicalism in achieving
social and political change.

Cogan, J & Derricott, R (2000)
Citizenship for the 21st Century: An International Perspective on Education, *Kogan Page*

Using case studies from Europe, Asia and North America this book reports on the findings of the Citizenship Education Policy Study which examines three vital questions. These are: i) What are the major global trends likely to have a significant impact on people's lives over the next 25 years? ii) What citizenship characteristics will people require in order to manage these trends? iii) How might such characteristics be developed through education? A timely, valuable and insightful international study.

Elkington, J & Hailes, J (1998)
Manual 2000: Life Choices for the Future you Want, *Hodder and Stoughton Limited*

Informed citizenship requires a basic understanding of contemporary social, environmental and scientific issues. It also requires an awareness of the moral dilemmas and lifestyle choices that such issues pose. This guide gives practical, up-to-date information and advice on available and affordable solutions to a range of current dilemmas. Topics covered include: the future we want; food and drink; community and home; transport and travel; communication and computers; money and investment; life and death.

Source: Reproduced by permission of Hodder and Stoughton Limited

Goalen, P (1999)
'...someone might become involved in a fascist group or something...', **Teaching History, Issue 96.**

This article, in a special issue of *Teaching History* on citizenship, reports on pupils' perceptions of history at the end of primary school and at secondary school. The author shows how, as a result of understanding the historical process, pupils are better able to tolerate different interpretations of the past. This acceptance of different interpretations is a vital element in the democratic process and can help underpin any notion of critical, active and reflective citizenship.

Hicks, D (1998)
'Exploring futures', **Chapter 20 in: Carter, R ed** ***Handbook of Primary Geography***, *Geographical Association*

One of the key concepts in geography is that of change. Some of the key questions that geography asks are: How is this place changing? How has it changed in the past? How may it change in the future? Who has the power to cause such changes? Who gains and who loses as a result? This chapter shows how an exploration of causes and consequences, probable and preferable futures is central to the process of geographical enquiry. Geography as a subject has a major role to play in helping promote more future-orientated citizenship.

Hicks, D & Holden, C (1995)
Visions of the Future: Why we Need to Teach for Tomorrow, *Trentham Books*

What are young people's hopes and fears for the future at personal, local and global scales? This book reports on the research that has been carried out in the UK and elsewhere on children's views of the future. It covers both the primary and secondary age range and gives detailed examples of their responses. Its importance lies in detailing the social and global concerns that young people themselves have in their own lives prior to any introduction to citizenship education.

Hicks, D & Slaughter, R eds (1998)
Futures Education: World Yearbook of Education 1998, *Kogan Page*

This book explains the need for, and origins of, a futures perspective in education. It does this using case studies at all levels of education from the USA, UK and Australia. The book is divided into three parts. The first looks at the nature of futures thinking and, in particular, the long established international field of futures studies. The second contains a wide range of illustrative case studies from schools and teacher education, which illustrate the actual practice of futures education. The third part looks at further innovative work that focuses on education for a sustainable future.

Holden, C & Clough, N eds (1998)
Children As Citizens: Education for Participation, *Jessica Kingsley*

Drawing on work carried out in Britain, other European countries and Australia, this book draws on the voices of children and classroom teachers to illustrate good practice in citizenship education. In particular the book shows how teachers can help develop young people's understanding of social justice, global responsibility, human rights and the rights of the child. Contributors also critically appraise citizenship education in relation to issues such as disability, economics, the environment, racism and power sharing in schools.

Hutchinson, F (1996)
Educating Beyond Violent Futures, *Routledge*

In this book Frank Hutchinson draws upon innovative research from wide ranging fields – sociology, peace and conflict studies, gender studies, media studies, futures studies and curriculum studies – in order to offer a vision of hope for the future. In investigating youth's views of the future, the author found that most teaching materials, games for young people and the media 'foreclose' on the future: that is, they offer very narrow and limited views of what is possible, doing little to challenge the materialist, patriarchal and often violent norms of Western society. Creative ways of challenging such assumptions are described

which need to be central to any notion of active citizenship.

May, G (1996)
The Future Is Ours: Foreseeing, Managing and Creating the Future, *Adamantine Press*

This is an excellent primer on futures thinking which explores both the difficulties and possibilities involved in thinking about, imagining and forecasting the future. The book explores the many ways in which humans try to conceptualise the future and exert control over it – generally, of course, unsuccessfully. It also explains the advantages of foresight and the ways in which this can be creatively used by experts and others to prepare more thoughtfully for a future which will be very different from today. An excellent detailed background to the futures field.

Oxfam (1997)
A Curriculum for Global Citizenship, *Oxfam*

This is a seminal document which takes the notion of citizenship and sets this firmly in a global context. Underpinning these guidelines is the belief that an education based on principles of equity and social justice, with the development of the global citizen at its heart, is the key to a sustainable future. Using the familiar headings of knowledge and understanding, skills, values and attitudes, a conceptual framework is set out which can then be directly related to school curriculum concerns. Official guidance on citizenship is incomplete without reference to this document. Oxfam also produces a *GC Link Bulletin* with up-to-date news on global citizenship issues.

Page, J (2000)
Reframing the Early Childhood Curriculum: Imperatives for the Future, *Routledge Falmer*

This book redresses a significant imbalance in research on early childhood education by demonstrating the need for a futures perspective in early years work. The purposes and principles of futures education are examined and shown to have much in common with the pre-existing aims of early childhood education. Whilst young children's attitudes towards the future and attendant notions of time and change are fundamentally different from those of adults, they nevertheless provide a fundamental foundation for personal growth, development and social learning.

'Focus on citizenship and the new national curriculum', *Primary Geographer,* **Number 40, January 2000 – special issue:**

Geography has a major role to play in citizenship education and this special issue highlights some of the possibilities at primary level. Articles include: 'Citizenship: concealed or revealed?'; 'Active infant citizens'; 'Our environment and transport'; 'Understanding before action'; and 'This democracy just isn't fair!'

SDEP (1999)
Sustainable Development Education Panel: First Annual Report, Department of Transport, Environment and Regions

Although produced as part of the English curriculum review process, this document does for education for sustainable development what the Oxfam document does for global citizenship. The focus of the panel is on lifelong learning in both formal and non-formal settings. Particular attention is paid here to work in primary and secondary schools and specific learning outcomes are suggested for knowledge, skills and values, at each key stage.

Wrenn, A (1999)
'Build it in, don't bolt it on: history's opportunity to support critical citizenship', *Teaching History,* **Issue 96.**

In this valuable and useful article, Wrenn argues that citizenship should not be seen as an imposition that history teachers have to deal with but rather as a valuable opportunity. History thus has a key role to play in citizenship education since it already deals with enquiry, interpretation, analysis, explanation and differing perspectives. These skills are also essential to the creation of informed citizens so that history's vital role in the curriculum can thus be strengthened.

JOURNALS

Ethical Consumer

ECRA Publishing Ltd, Unit 21, 41 Old Birley Street, Manchester M15 5RF. Tel: (0161) 226 2929; web site: www.ethicalconsumer.org

An excellent magazine which highlights a wide range of consumer issues. There are detailed reports in each edition on various products, ranging from insurance and breakfast cereals to baby food and washing up liquids. Different brands are assessed in relation to company policies on the environment, animal testing, workers rights, armaments, genetic engineering and oppressive regimes. Excellent illustrations of local-global connections and citizen action for change.

Green Futures

Circa, 13-17 Sturton Street, Cambridge CB1 2SN. Tel: (01223) 564334; email: greenfutures@circa-uk.demon.co.uk

This well illustrated and informative journal comes from Forum for the Future and provides up-to-date reports on progress towards sustainable development in all sectors of society. No prior knowledge of sustainability issues is required for these short accounts of environmental and social best practice which illustrate how business, local authorities, government and education are successfully beginning to rise to the challenge of creating a more sustainable future. Good illustrations and contact details. An excellent resource on sustainability in action.

New Internationalist

Tower House, Lathkill Street, Market Harborough LE16 9EF. Tel: (01858) 439616; web site: www.newint.org/

Each month this magazine gives an overview of a major world issue ranging from climate change, mining, bananas, and poverty to Indonesia, the radical 20th century and redesigning the global economy. An excellent and informative resource for both the individual teacher and the school library.

Resurgence

Rocksea Farmhouse, St Mabyn, Bodmin, Cornwall PL30 3BR. Tel: (01208) 841824; web site: www.resurgence.org

One of the UK's leading magazines dealing with green and environmental issues, it describes itself as an international forum for ecological and spiritual thinking. Includes articles by leading social and global visionaries on all aspects of transformative change, on the arts and crafts, as well as book reviews and details of courses and conferences at Schumacher College in Devon.

ADDRESSES

Birmingham Development Education Centre

998 Bristol Road, Selly Oak, Birmingham B29 6LE. Tel: (0121) 472 3255; web site: www.tidec.org

Birmingham DEC works in partnership with teachers and schools to bring a global dimension and a development perspective to the curriculum. This partnership is known as Tide (Teachers In Development Education). The Centre maintains a good stock of development education resources for sale and details are available in the Tide catalogue. The Centre has an excellent reputation for its teacher produced resources.

Citizenship Foundation

15 St Swithin's Lane, London EC4N 8AL. Tel: (020) 7929 3344; web site: www.citfou.org.uk

The Citizenship Foundation promotes Citizenship education through a wide range of programmes, particularly in relation to: law and the legal system; human rights; education for democracy; and moral and critical thinking. A range of publications is available for primary and secondary schools and the Foundation also has considerable in-service expertise.

The Centre for Citizenship Studies in Education

University of Leicester, School of Education, 21 University Road, Leicester LE1 7RF. Tel: (0116) 252 3681; web site: www.le.ac.uk/education/centres/citizenship

The Centre exists to promote citizenship education in schools through collaboration with teachers, schools and other partners. It has an on-going programme of publications, research, consultancy, in-service, courses and conferences. It also acts as a clearing house for recording, exchange and dissemination of information relating to citizenship education.

The Centre for Global Education

University College of Ripon and York, Lord Mayor's Walk, York YO3 7EX. Tel: (01904) 656771; email: Global.ed@dial.pipex.com

The Centre is an interdisciplinary, curriculum development centre which supports primary and secondary teachers in introducing global issues into the classroom. Current and recent projects include: Development Education through the Teaching of Spanish; Human Rights in the Curriculum; Literacy, Global Awareness and Citizenship in the Early Years; Global Education Summer Schools. The Centre also edits the quarterly *Human Rights Education* Newsletter.

Institute for Citizenship

62 Marylebone High Street, London W1M 3AF. Tel: (020) 7935 4777; web site: www.citizen.org.uk/

The aim of the Institute is to promote informed active citizenship and greater participation in democracy and society. The Institute has a particular interest in citizenship education and has developed and piloted various curriculum projects, including useful resources for teachers on citizenship at infant, junior and secondary levels.

Manchester Development Education Project

c/o Manchester Metropolitan University, 801 Wilmslow Road, Didsbury, Manchester M20 2QR. Tel: (0161) 445 2495; web site: www.dep.org.uk/

DEP provides a wide range of services to schools on world events, development issues and global citizenship. These include a resource centre and bookshop with mail order facilities; in-service training for teachers; curriculum development projects, and their own educational publications. Resource lists are available on themes such as: citizenship; education for sustainable development; bullying; race; gender; disability; and school curriculum subject areas.

Oxfam

274 Banbury Road, Oxford OX2 7DZ. Tel: (01865) 311311; web site: www.oxfam.org.uk/coolplanet/

Oxfam's catalogue on education resources for schools is a treasure chest of information on innovative teachers' packs, books, videos, maps, posters and games on global issues. These cover all aspects of the school curriculum and all age groups. The teachers' web site can be accessed via the web site for children listed above.

WWF-UK

Panda House, Weyside Park, Godalming, Surrey GU7 1XR. Tel: (01483) 426444; main web site: www.wwf-uk.org or visit the dedicated education site at www.wwflearning.co.uk

WWF-UK's education catalogue features some 200 teaching/learning resource for schools in the form of teachers' handbooks, posters, multimedia packs, educational software and children's readers – all with an education for sustainable development angle, and many with citizenship content. Resources have been developed to cover all aspects of the school curriculum and all age groups. Their dedicated, interactive education website also offers a news service, resources (online and to download), exhibition rooms and discussion forums.

All I ever really needed to know I learned in kindergarten

Most of what I really need to know about how to live, and what to do, and how to be, I learned in kindergarten. Wisdom was not at the top of the graduate school mountain, but there in the sandbox at nursery school.

These are the things I learned: Share everything. Play fair. Don't hit people. Put things back where you found them. Clean up your own mess. Don't take things that aren't yours. Say you're sorry when you hurt somebody. Wash your hands before you eat. Flush. Warm cookies and cold milk are good for you. Live a balanced life. Learn some and think some and draw and paint and sing and dance and play and work every day some.

Take a nap every afternoon. When you go into the world, watch for traffic, hold hands and stick together. Be aware of wonder. Remember the little seed in the plastic cup. The roots go down and the plant goes up and nobody really knows how or why, but we are all like that.

Goldfish and hamsters and white mice and even the little seed in the plastic cup – they all die. So do we.

And then remember the book about Dick and Jane and the first word you learned, the biggest word of all: LOOK. Everything you need to know is in there somewhere. The Golden Rule and love and basic sanitation. Ecology and politics and sane living.

Think of what a better world it would be if we all – the whole world – had cookies and milk about 3 o'clock every afternoon and then lay down with our blankets for a nap. Or if we had a basic policy in our nation and other nations always to put things back where we found them, and cleaned up our own messes. And it is still true, no matter how old you are, when you go out into the world, it is best to hold hands and stick together.

Source: *All I ever really needed to know I learned at kindergarten*, Robert Fulghum, Villard Books, 1988

References

Chapter 1

1 Toffler, A (1974) *Learning for Tomorrow: The Role of the Future in Education*, New York: Vintage Books/Random House.

2 Hicks, D & Holden, C eds (1995) *Visions of the Future: Why We Need to Teach for Tomorrow*, Stoke-on-Trent: Trentham Books; Hutchinson, F (1996) *Educating Beyond Violent Futures*, London: Routledge.

3 Hicks & Holden (as above).

4 Brown, L, Renner, M & Halweil, B (1999) *Vital Signs: The Environmental Signs that are Shaping our Future*, London: Earthscan.

5 Pike, G & Selby, D (1988) *Global Teacher, Global Learner*, London: Hodder & Stoughton (pp1-3)

6 Fox, M (1994) *The Reinvention of Work: A New Vision of Livelihood for our Time*, New York: Harper SanFrancisco.

7 Hicks, D & Slaughter, R eds (1998) *Futures Education: World Yearbook of Education 1998*, London: Kogan Page.

8 Coleman, S & O'Sullivan eds (1990) *William Morris and News From Nowhere: A Vision for our Time*, Bideford: Green Books.

9 SDEP (1999) *Sustainable Development Education Panel: First Annual Report 1998*, London: Department of the Environment, Transport and Regions; Huckle, J & Sterling, S eds (1996) *Education for Sustainability*, London: Earthscan.

10 Useful periodicals with examples of positive action for change include: *Green Futures, Ethical Consumer, New Internationalist, Resurgence* (see Chapter 8 for details).

11 Capra, F (1983) *The Turning Point: Science, Society and the Rising Culture*, London: Fontana.

12 Milbrath, L (1989) *Envisioning a Sustainable Society: Learning our Way Out*, Albany: State University of New York; Inglehart, R (1997) *Modernisation and Postmodernization: Cultural, Economic, and Political Change in 43 Societies*, Princeton NJ: Princeton University Press.

Chapter 2

1 DfEE/QCA (1999) *The National Curriculum: Handbook for Primary/Secondary Teachers in England*, London: Department for Environment and Education/Qualifications and Curriculum Authority.

2 LT Scotland (2000) 'The Structure and Balance of the Curriculum', *5–14 National Guidelines*, Learning and Teaching Scotland

3 DfEE/QCA (1999) *Citizenship: Key Stages 3–4*, London: Department for Environment and Education/Qualifications and Curriculum Authority.

4 LT Scotland (September 2000) *Education for Citizenship: A Paper for Discussion and Consultation*, Learning and Training Scotland.

5 Richardson, R (1990) *Daring to be a Teacher: Essays, Stories and Memoranda*, Stoke-on-Trent: Trentham Books.

6 LT Scotland (2000) 'Environmental Studies – Society, Science and Technology', *5–14 National Guidelines*, Learning and Teaching Scotland

7 DfEE/QCA (1999) *The National Curriculum: Handbook for Primary/Secondary Teachers in England*, London: Department for Environment and Education/Qualifications and Curriculum Authority.

8 Kerr, D (1999) *Re-examining Citizenship Education: The Case of England*, Slough: National Foundation for Educational Research.

9 Oxfam (1997) *A Curriculum for Global Citizenship*, Oxford: Oxfam.

10 Cogan, J & Derricott, R (2000) *Citizenship for the 21st Century: An International Perspective on Education*, London: Kogan Page.

11 As 9 above.

12 Pike, G & Selby, D (1996) *Reconnecting: From National to Global Curriculum*, Godalming: WWF-UK

13 Hicks, D & Slaughter, R eds (1998) *Futures Education: World Yearbook of Education 1998*, London: Kogan Page.

Chapter 5

1 Huckle, J (1990) 'Consuming interests', in NALGO Education, *Greenprint for Action: A Course on the Key Environmental Issues of the 1990s*, Cambridge: National Extension College.

2 Quoted in Hicks, D & Steiner, M eds (1989) *Making Global Connections: A World Studies Workbook*, Harlow: Oliver & Boyd.

3 Pearce, D *et al* (1989) *Blueprint for a Green Economy*, London: Earthscan.

4 See Chapter 10 in Macy, J & Brown, M (1998) *Coming Back to Life: Practices to Reconnect our Lives, our World*, Gabriola BC: New Society Publishers.

REFERENCES

Chapter 6

1 Fowles, J (1987) *Handbook of Futures Research*, London: Greenwood Press.

2 Quotations taken from: Berger, J (1990) *The Gaia Atlas of First Peoples*, London: Robertson McCarta.

Chapter 8

1 Gough, N (1990) 'Futures in Australian education – tacit, token and taken for granted', *Futures*, 22 (3), April.

2 Storm, M (1991) 'Fixes for the future', *Times Educational Supplement*, 15 November.

Acknowledgements

Many teachers, advisers and inspectors helped in the evolution of this book which first appeared in an earlier version entitled *Educating for the Future* (WWF-UK, 1994). They include: David Barrs, Veronique Buckingham, Amber Carroll, Annamarie de Chiara, Fiona Cooper, Pete Coulson, Marta Fontana, David Ferns, Catherine Foxon, Colin Harris, Frank Holman, Kath Iglesias, Laura Galletti, David Gamble, Mike Hillary, Prue Poulton, Anne Reyersbach, Adriana de Rossi, John Scamons, Neil Sledge, Maurice Smith, John Stewart, Glenn Strachan, David Thomas, Lisa Webb and Paul Webber.

More recently I am indebted to: Roy Blatchford and the staff at Walton High in Milton Keynes for inviting me to run an Advanced Learning Day on 'Choosing the Future'; all the students at Bath Spa University College who over the years have taken ED381H Futures Education; Rupert Maclean who invited me to give the keynote lecture at the fifth UNESCO-ACEID international conference in Bangkok; my always supportive colleagues, Kay Wood and Andy Bord, in International Education; Cathie Holden at Exeter University for her timely information and encouragement; Patrick Whitaker for his unfaltering personal and professional support; Rick Slaughter at Swinburne University in Australia for being the first Professor of Foresight; and staff at WWF for capably seeing this book through its latest lifecycle.

Appendix

The key elements for responsible Global Citizenship

Social justice & equity

Understanding of inequality and injustice within and between societies. Knowledge of basic human needs and rights and of our responsibilities as Global Citizens.

Critical thinking

Ability to assess viewpoints and information in an open-minded and critical way and to be able to change one's opinions, challenge one's own assumptions and make ethical judgements as a result.

Globalisation and interdependence

Knowledge about the world and its affairs: the links between countries, power relationships and different political systems. An understanding of the complexities of global issues.

Peace and conflict

Understanding of historical and present day conflicts and conflict mediation and prevention.

Skills

Ability to argue effectively

Ability to find out information and to present an informed, persuasive argument based on reason.

Knowledge and understanding

Co-operation and conflict resolution

Ability to share and to work with others effectively, to analyse conflicts objectively and to find resolutions acceptable to all sides.

Sustainable development

Knowledge of how to take care of things. A recognition that the Earth's resources are finite, precious and unequally used. An understanding of the global imperative of sustainable development.

Diversity

Understanding of cultural and other diversity within societies and how the lives of others can enrich our own. Knowledge of the nature of prejudice towards diversity and how it can be combated.

Empathy
Sensitivity to the feelings, needs and lives of others in the world; a sense of common humanity and common needs and rights. A capacity for compassion.

Sense of identity and self-esteem
A feeling of one's own value and individuality.

Ability to challenge injustice and inequalities
Ability to recognise injustice and inequality in whatever form it is met and to select appropriate action.

Belief that people can make a difference
A realisation that individuals can act to improve situations and a desire to participate and take action.

Values and attitudes

Value and respect for diversity
Appreciation that everyone is different but equal and that we can learn from each other.

Concern for the environment and commitment to sustainable development
Respect and concern for the environment and all life within it. A willingness to consider the needs of future generations and to act responsibly.

Commitment to social justice and equity
An interest in and concern about global issues; commitment to fairness and readiness to work for a more just world.

Source: Oxfam (1997) *A Curriculum for Global Citizenship*, Oxfam

Global Citizenship: knowledge and understanding

Knowledge and understanding	Social justice and equity	Diversity	Globalisation and interdependence	Sustainable development	Peace and Conflict
Pre KS1 Pre stages P1-P3	• What is fair/unfair • What is right and wrong	• Awareness of others in relation to self • Awareness of similarities and differences between people	• Sense of immediate and local environment • Awareness of different places	• Living things and their needs • How to take care of things • A sense of the future	• Our actions have consequences
KS1 Stages P1-P3	• Awareness of rich and poor	• Greater awareness of similarities and differences between people	• Sense of the wider world • Links and connections between different places	• Our impact on the environment • Awareness of the past and the future	• Conflicts past and present in our society and others • Causes of conflict and conflict resolution – personal level
KS2 Stages P4-P6	• Fairness between groups • Causes and effects of inequality	• Contribution of different cultures, values and beliefs to our lives • Nature of prejudice and ways to combat it	• Trade between countries • Fair trade	• Relationship between people and environment • Awareness of finite resources • Our potential to change things	• Causes of conflict • Impact of conflict strategies for tackling conflict and for conflict prevention
KS3 Stages P7-S2	• Inequalities within and between societies • Basic rights and responsibilities	• Understanding of issues of diversity	• Awareness of interdependence • Our political system and others	• Different views of economic and social development, locally and globally • Understanding the concepts of possible and preferable futures	• Causes and effects of conflict, local and globally • Relationship between conflict and peace
LS4 S3-Standard grade	• Causes of poverty • Different views on the eradication of poverty • Role as Global Citizen	• Deeper understanding of different cultures and societies	• Power relationships • North/South • World economic and political systems • Ethical consumerism	• Global imperative of sustainable development • Lifestyles for a sustainable world	• Conditions conducive to peace
16-19	• Understanding of global debates	• Deeper understanding of different cultures and societies	• Complexity of global issues	• Understanding of key issues of Agenda 21 • Lifestyles for a sustainable world	• Complexity of conflict issues and conflict resolution

Source: Oxfam (1997) *A Curriculum for Global Citizenship*, Oxfam

Global Citizenship: skills

Skills	Critical thinking	Ability to argue effectively	Ability to challenge injustice and inequalities	Respect for people and things	Co-operation and conflict resolution
Pre KS1 Pre stages P1-P3	• Listening to others • Asking questions	• Expressing a view	• Beginning to identify unfairness and take appropriate action	• Starting to take care of things – animate and inanimate • Starting to think of others	• Co-operating • Sharing • Starting to look at resolving arguments peacefully • Starting to participate
KS1 Stages P1-P3	• Looking at different viewpoints • Developing an enquiring mind	• Beginning to stage an opinion based on evidence	• Beginning to identify unfairness and take appropriate action	• Empathising and responding to the needs of others • Making links between our lives and the lives of others	• Tact and diplomacy • Involving/including society and others
KS2 Stages P4-P6	• Detecting bias, opinion and stereotypes • Assessing different viewpoints	• Finding and selecting evidence • Beginning to present a reasoned case	• Recognising and starting to challenge unfairness	• Making choices and recognising the consequences of choices	• Accepting and acting on group decisions • Compromising
KS3 Stages P7-S2	• Media literacy • Making informed decisions	• Learning to develop/change position through reasoned argument	• Starting to challenge viewpoints which perpetuate inequality	• Growing ability to take care of things – animate and inanimate	• Negotiation
LS4 S3-Standard grade	• Critically analysing information • Making ethical judgement	• Arguing rationally and persuasively from an informed position	• Selecting appropriate action to take against inequality	• Following a personal lifestyle for a sustainable world	• Negotiation • Mediation
16-19	• Handling contentious and complex issues	• Political literacy • Participating in relevant political processes	• Campaigning for a more just and equitable world	• Following a personal lifestyle for a sustainable world	• Negotiation • Conflict resolution

Source: Oxfam (1997) *A Curriculum for Global Citizenship*, Oxfam

Global Citizenship: values and attitudes

Values and attitudes	Sense of identify and self-esteem	Empathy and sense of common humanity	Commitment to social justice and equity	Valuing and respecting diversity	Concern for the environment and commitment to sustainable development	Belief that people can make a difference
Pre KS1 Pre stages P1-P3	• Sense of identity and self-worth	• Concern for others in immediate circle	• Sense of fair play	• Positive attitude towards difference and diversity	• Appreciation of own environment and living things • Sense of wonder and curiosity	• Willingness to admit to and learn from mistakes
KS1 Stages P1-P3	• Awareness of and pride in individuality	• Interest and concern for others in wider sphere	• Sense of personal indignation • Willingness to speak up for others	• Valuing others as equal and different • Willingness to learn from the experiences of others	• Concern for the wider environment • Beginning to value resources • Willingness to care for the environment	• Awareness that our actions have consequences • Willingness to co-operate and participate
KS2 Stages P4-P6	• Sense of importance of individual worth	• Empathy towards others locally and globally	• Growing interest in world events • Sense of justice	• Growing respect for difference and diversity	• Sense of responsibility for the environment and the use of resources	• Belief that things can be better and that individuals can make a difference
KS3 Stages P7-S2	• Open-mindedness	• Compassion • Sensitivity to the needs and rights of others	• Concern for injustice and inequality • Willingness to take action against inequality	• Respecting rights of all to have a point of view	• Concern about the effects of our lifestyles on people and the environment	• Willingness to take a stand on global issues
LS4 S3-Standard grade	• Open-mindedness	• Sense of common humanity and common needs	• Commitment to social justice and equity	• Valuing all people as equal and different	• Concern for the future of the planet and future generations • Commitment to a lifestyle for a sustainable world	• Willingness to work towards a more equitable future
16-19	• Open-mindedness	• Sense of individual and collective responsibility	• Commitment to the eradication of poverty	• Valuing all people as equal and different	• Commitment to sustainable development	• Willingness to work towards a more equitable future

Source: Oxfam (1997) A Curriculum for Global Citizenship, Oxfam